SKY-HITCHING TO HEAVEN

Experiencing the Fun Side of God

MARY L. GORDON

© 2024 Mary L. Gordon. All rights reserved
ISBN 979-8-9903674-4-9
Cover Design: Nusrat Abbas Awan
www.skyhitchingtoheaven.com

Contents

Acknowledgments

I am so grateful for so many people who have been a part of this book. It would be impossible to name them all, but here are a few.

First of all, God Himself provided all the experiences I've described. Without Him, none of this would even have happened. I'm so thankful to have such a wonderful God.

Of course, I'm super grateful to my husband, Ron Gordon, who has patiently given me the time I needed to write. He also has been an encourager and critic for me.

There were times I thought this material wasn't worth the effort, but then I'd remember my friend Jill Benson who read the original rough draft. She wasn't planning to read it all at once, but as she explained, after she got to a certain point, she was "all in" and finished the entire book in one night. That has kept me encouraged.

Next are all the characters you will meet. I'm grateful to every one of them for being in my life. In chapter one you will meet Barbara Parlow who has always been an encouraging friend.

I am wildly thankful for Graham Cooke and other ministers who have acquainted us with the God of wonder, the God who often seems too good to be true.

Thank you also, Pedro Adao, for encouraging me to get to work and produce all that God has put within me. Much of what I've accomplished through writing in the last year and a half was only in seed form until I began to participate in your movement.

Also a special shout-out to my book coach, Christine Gail, CEO and best-selling author of Unleash Your Rising® and to my editor, Mary Jo Rennert Gremling, CEO of Bestwine Press.

Preface

Not only is God real, He's a blast. How many of you have actually experienced His personality? I doubt there are many, and that's why I decided to write down some of the wild experiences I've enjoyed with a real God who not only talks to me, but who also delights in what I do.

God is the one responsible for many of my craziest ideas. Also, He has always been with me when I carry them out. He goes on my adventures with me and then provides special events of enjoyment in the process.

Oh, how I wish others could see the brilliance of such a powerful Entity! I want others to be able to rave as much as I have.

My greatest desire is that you will take these incidents to heart and decide to get to know Him better. I know for sure He wants that for you.

Introduction

My life has been rich with lots of whitewater, canoeing, training dogs, camping in snow, and sky-hitching from mid-Ohio to Washington state, to name a few. I've seen God in all of it, and I can testify that boredom is not in the picture.

God was never the stodgy religious fellow up in the sky who pours out condemnation and judgment on everything we do. In fact, He has often been the instigator of my experiences that turned into wild escapades.

I met Jesus in 1975, and that elevated my life into another plane altogether. I noticed that God made the fun times more enjoyable, the adventures more adventurous, and the serious times more enriching.

In this book, I share the fun things that happened to me. Of course, that doesn't mean I leave God out, but I want these incidents to be pleasurable reading for believers and non-believers alike.

Each chapter is a stand-alone story, and you can feel free to skip around. In fact, if you are not an outdoors person, I won't be insulted if you skip a camping chapter entirely.

Over the years, I continually wrote detailed letters to my friends about how God was showing off. I also made copies of the letters and named that collection "My Diary." This has left me with a wealth of recorded material. If it were not for all those wonderful friends, I would not have the reliable sources necessary to claim all this is true. However, I can validate every detail in these stories except that I've changed some of the names.

As you join me in my adventures, you will not only see a real God, but also an amusing side of Him you might never have realized. If everyone knew how much fun He can be, maybe they'd be more interested in getting to know Him. I sure hope so.

Unless otherwise noted, all quoted Scripture is from the King James Version (KJV).

Mary L. Gordon

01

Are You One of Them?

"My eyes had been closed, and when I opened them, there in front of me was the most shocking sight."

Back in 1995, my husband Ron and I were visiting a friend in Kentucky. It was during a time when I was super gung-ho to spend time talking to Jesus as often as possible.

On a bright sunshiny morning, I took a walk to the site of a future housing project, found a pile of discarded overgrown rocks, and climbed up on top. It was early spring, and a nearby young tree was still bare branched.

As I was praying, something very unusual happened. My eyes had been closed, and when I opened them, there in front of me was the most shocking sight. I saw at least seven or eight birds, all of different colors—all on that one very short tree. There was a blue jay, a cardinal, a black bird, a robin, one that was bright yellow, and others of equal diversity. When one or two flew away, two or three others would land. All of them were different from each other.

Oh my! What did this mean? It was so untypical; there had to be something Jesus intended for me to learn. When I pondered it, the thought came that He was showing me the diversity of the people I would reach.

In 2022, my friend Barbara visited and brought a picture she had painted for me. She knew nothing of my previous prayer experiences. When she showed me her painting, I saw only blotches of reds, blues, blacks, and greens. But upon gazing at it further, I realized it was a picture of many birds. She confirmed that birds were what she had intended.

Birds by Barbara Parlow

We both rejoiced after I shared my prayer incident with the birds, knowing that she had painted a prophetic picture for me. Now, when

I look at her artwork, I'm reminded of that day when God showed me there would be a diversity of people I'd reach.

I guess you are one of them.

Fun Time

Have you ever had a notion to give something to someone when it didn't make any sense? It could be God working in you, and it's really fun to carry it out and see what God has in mind.

It's Dry on the Porch

"After he left, I suddenly felt assured that the people wouldn't be back— it had to be God's revelation."

In September of 1978, I was moving from a year-long assignment of work in northwestern Ohio. It was the final year of my Biblical leadership training, and I would be starting out at a small campus in northeastern Indiana north of Fort Wayne. To make the move from Ohio to Indiana, a friend of mine named Michael, and I decided to ride our ten-speed bicycles. Here's a detailed description of the trip.

Our brief adventure was a big success. One time right after we crossed into Indiana, we passed a house where somebody had strewn toilet paper over all the trees and flowers, and I took a notion to clean up the mess. I noticed a guy sitting and working in the garage, and I struck up an enjoyable conversation with him while admiring some lovely re-upholstery work he was doing. He claimed that the only thing God promised was salvation, and I countered him, claiming that God met all of our needs.

Just as we were leaving, I heard a scraping against the back wheel of my bike. The man jumped up, immediately recognized the problem, and replaced a missing bolt from my rack. Then I said, "Who says God doesn't meet needs? Look at the detail!"

What if I hadn't stopped? All my gear rested upon that rack which could have collapsed. That would have been disastrous! I met that worker because I followed a nudge to clean up a mess. Today we call that a random act of kindness.

In Fort Wayne, we decided to stop and visit a friend. Once we were comfortably situated in his home, a big rainstorm started. How about that timing?

Michael and I Ready to Ride

Michael and I dramatically saw how God can work with two people. What a joy! Sunday evening, we left Ft. Wayne, and God revealed to me to ask at a farm to camp on the property. After a while,

I mentioned it to Michael and then got concerned that since I shared it, the adversary would try to trick us into staying at a lousy place.

My belief was that as long as my request was locked in my mind, it was a secret between God and me. But since Michael was my riding partner, I couldn't leave him out.

God knew my thoughts and gave me my next realization. If God independently revealed the same farm to each of us separately, that revelation would be doubled, thus established. That was my reasoning, (based on a verse in Genesis).

> *And for that the dream was doubled unto Pharaoh twice;*
> *it is because the thing is established by God, and God will*
> *shortly bring it to pass.*
>
> Genesis 41:32

Not long afterward, we rode by a very nice-looking place, but Michael didn't say anything so I continued on ahead. Finally, Michael shouted up to me, "Hey, Mary, what about this place?" Then I was sure it was right. We went up to the house to ask, but no one was home. However, we had supper there by the roadside, and then a man showed up to do some chores at the farm.

He assured us we could stay there, but he also added that the owner was a mean one and would be home that night. After he left, I suddenly felt assured that the people would not be back—it had to be God's revelation. So we moved onto the front porch and stayed dry while it thundered and poured all night.

The owner will never know.

Fun Time

Has there been a time when you knew in your gut something to be true, and yet you didn't act accordingly? What if that gut-knowing was revelation from God?

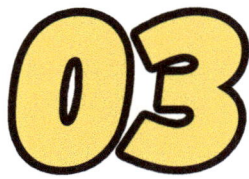

A Small-Town Adventure

"We entered the house, found a stairway upstairs, located his bedroom, and woke him up."

One of the exercises in my Biblical leadership training was called "Lightbearers." In this exercise we'd go to some assigned town, talk to people about God, the Bible, etc., and register as many as possible for our Bible class.

We had no idea where we would stay, as we were expected to trust God for everything. We had some money but not enough for more than one night if we went to a motel (which back then cost around $20).

The first time I wrote about this incident, I cried for joy,. noting how God has always taken care of me, and never let me down.

We went in pairs, and we were sent where there were not yet any known believers. My partner was named K, and we hitchhiked to our assigned town south of Wichita, Kansas. It was late afternoon when we arrived, and what we had to our advantage was the Bible and a specific technique of how to share it. We also had something else going for us: our like-mindedness. We had agreed together to get up at 4 a.m., pray, jog, and study God's word before the day began.

When we got to town, we entered a drugstore to get something for K. We had practiced starting conversations with a compliment and then leading from the complimentary topic to questions like "Why does this quality in your life make a difference?" or "Why is this important to you?" The object was to find out what a person really wanted and why.

I approached the proprietor of the drugstore, and proceeded to try out our method right off. I found something on which to compliment her, and that led to her telling us about a time she had gotten healed. Then I was able to reach her heart with a compliment regarding how she had been believing and doing exactly what the Bible teaches us about how to receive. The conversation took a turn. She wanted to know everything about us—why we were there, how long we were staying, where we were going to stay, where we were headed right then, etc.

We informed her that we planned to get some groceries and go to a park to fix our supper. Then we'd find a motel for one night, but if she knew anyone we could stay with, we would be very thankful. We left her store after she made sure of our plans. K and I felt certain that she would help us, but we were schooled about trusting God and not man.

We had a deep sense of believing she would reach out to us, so we hung around the park until almost dark hoping she'd show up. But the park remained lifeless except for one guy, and our conversation with him was not profitable. Then a car with a bunch of young people drove close by, and some guy hollered at us. We weren't convinced of his motive, and after they left, we decided that we should get on with it and hitchhike to a motel.

We were just in the process of registering when the craziest thing happened. I had already filled out the registration form and had a $20 bill in my hand. I was holding it out to the clerk, when the phone rang at the motel. The clerk kept looking at us as she answered questions posed by the person on the other end of the line, and then she handed the red receiver to me. It was our drugstore friend. She had a place for us, and she came and picked us up. It turned out to be the third floor of her own home—a whole apartment with a kitchen and bathroom. She needed to talk it over with her husband before letting us know about it. WOW.

She had been calling around to every motel in the phonebook to find us. We also learned that she had sent that car full of young people to the park, but they weren't mature enough to filter through our concerns regarding their intentions.

And get this: after we had been in that apartment for a couple of days, this lady offered us the use of their camping van, a VW Microbus. Now we had wheels.

When we hitchhiked to the motel, K had left her Bible in some guy's truck. Check this out! We got her Bible back, and here's how. God is so faithful and amazing. That guy had shown some interest in God's Word when he drove us, and K had his address.

Sunday morning we went to his home. Nobody came to the door when we knocked. The screen door was closed, but the main door was standing open. We agreed together that the family had gone to church, and our guy was still sleeping. That was actually God's revelation, but we had to dare to believe it. We entered the house, found a stairway, located his bedroom, and woke him up. After he overcame his shock at finding us standing by his bedside, he was again receptive to the gospel, and K got her Bible.

I still am awed by how I've dared to believe God in the physical realm, and I realize I can trust Him just as much in the emotional realm. He's the same God, and He meets all our needs. Look how He took care of K and me! The very first person we spoke with gave us a free apartment in which to stay as well as the use of one of her vehicles. Imagine that!

It worked both ways. Our host couple's marriage had gotten somewhat tense, so we invited them upstairs to a romantic dinner for two, complete with candlelight and the works. We had a blast cooking the meal and serving it to them. Our hostess was very thankful.

Fun Time

Do you believe that God wants to take care of you and meet every need you have? What action on your part would open a pathway to His care?

04

A Fairy Tale Experience at the Farm

"... and he, too, didn't have anyone else with whom to set up a car shuttle."

The week had finally arrived. It was October 12, 1986, when Ron planned to fulfill a promise he had made to me when we got married. I was excited too. We were going camping; in fact, we were going backpacking. We would be away from our car and all roads for three days of hiking on the Laurel Highlands Trail in western Pennsylvania.

I had looked forward to this trip even more than to our wedding the previous April. I love the outdoors; I love to cook over campfires; I love gathering wood; I love the fresh air all night long; I love it all.

This was it. We were going. And it drizzled all the way to the trail. Ugh. Rain is not my favorite weather for all this activity, but it was too late to find a different week.

Fortunately, before we left, Ron noted that we might want to go canoeing as well, so we had our boat on the car. And since it was rainy, why not paddle on day one and save the hiking for afterward?

We really didn't know how we were going to manage this whole canoeing trip. One really needs two cars—one for each end of the trip. The only thing I could figure was to have Ron drop me, the canoe, and all the gear off where we'd begin paddling, and then he would take the car to the other end, and somehow get back to me.

That might not be such an easy task. It was a Monday, and there probably wouldn't be much traffic on those country mountain roads. On the way to the river, I started to get really anxious—especially after observing three vans loaded with kayaks going in the opposite direction. I wondered if there were a better place to go where we'd find other boaters who could help us get set up.

Now, God gets to show off. Just as we were pulling away from the last town I noticed a boating and wilderness outfitter's place right along the highway and said, "Ron, stop." He pulled over, and just then a guy came walking out of the front door of the store. I said to him, "Do you know anyone paddling on the Youghiogheny River today?" He replied, "Which section?" I said, "The middle section," and he said, "Which put in?"

This was too much. He wanted to paddle on the same section, and he, too, didn't have anyone else with whom to set up a car shuttle. Then he opened up what was to develop into magnificent fellowship with the comment, "You know, you're really an answer to prayer." Well, our reply dumbfounded him, and then he informed us that he had prayed that morning, specifically, that he would find Christians to paddle with!! Can you believe it?

Later in the afternoon when the river tamed down to a lazy flow, Ron and I sang duets for him. The mountains rose up out of the river on both sides in full fall colors, and our new friend, Vernon, could not rave enough about it when we reached the end of the trip.

But God was showing off even more than we knew. Vernon had

driven to the area two days earlier on Saturday, and attended a local church on Sunday. He had prayed with a family he met at the church, and was invited to park his camper at their house Sunday night. When he met us on Monday, he gave us their name and address. I had planned to cook our supper at our campsite, but I knew most firewood would be soaked. Vernon was driving a camper, and although he originally had planned to drive home earlier, he had a stove, and we had lots of food, so we enjoyed supper together. That was too super!

Ron and I were looking forward to the backpacking, fully expecting the weather to be clear, but we were concerned about where to leave our car, especially with a canoe on top, while we were on the trail. That's when I thought of calling those people Vernon had told us about. I introduced myself on the phone as the answer to the prayer they had prayed with Vernon before he left to go boating on Monday.

I talked with the mother, and she was enthusiastic about helping us out. We said we'd finish packing and then come down to meet her. Then she would take us to the trail, keep our car at their farm, and pick us up on Friday at noon. She was very receptive to our Biblical conversation, and we thoroughly enjoyed our fellowship with her that afternoon.

Not only that, but the family had a piano that needed tuning. We had planned to pay them for their trouble, but Ron had his piano tuning tools in the trunk, and that was worth quite a bit to them since they lived out in the middle of nowhere. She said she drove her daughter more than a half hour each way for piano lessons each week. When we got off the trail around noon on Friday, Ron tuned their piano.

En route to the beginning of our hike, the clouds nearly disappeared, and we enjoyed beautiful sunshine on those gorgeous leaves, not only then, but for the next three days while we walked. But there was a problem.

We had barely hiked a mile or two when my back began to complain to me. I had no history of back pain, and this simply could not be happening. I had been looking forward to this trip for a very long time.

Here's a benefit of having the spirit of God living inside. I knew a lot of Scripture, and the verse that came to mind at that time was one that promised healing.

> *Beloved, I wish above all things that thou mayest prosper and be in health, even as thy soul prospereth.*
>
> 3 John 2

I quoted it out loud. I quoted it again. And again and again, up to about a hundred times. I was determined and adamant, and the pain left!!

(But only for a few minutes, and then it returned.)

Argh. I wasn't about to give up this trip. "Well," I decided, "it worked once; it'll work again." So I began to quote that same verse again, over and over, and that second time it only took about fifty rounds before the pain left. And it never came back.

You guys—yeah you, the ones reading this—do you doubt this all happened exactly as I'm relating it? It's hard to get your mind around it, but that's just the thing. God is so gracious and good, it can seem like a fairy tale sometimes, but this is what really happened. If I had any idea how to contact Vernon or that family at this point, I'd have them testify.

We camped at shelter areas, which were abundant, and we had no trouble finding dry wood. All the shelters had fireplaces, and at one of them, I kept the fire going all night long. It was sweet.

In the meantime, the family had agreed that we could have a small Bible meeting in their home on Friday night. Vernon had returned from Pittsburgh, so he was present also. Ron shared on the topic of believing, and we sang some songs. It was a great evening that could have lasted all night if we hadn't gotten so sleepy. They had several guest rooms, so we all stayed at the farm.

They had four children, and I was impressed by how they'd

masterfully raised them to be well-behaved and respectful to both of their parents.

Now for a couple more fun details. During our hike, Ron continually reminded me about a gallon of Pennsylvania maple syrup we had purchased. He wanted to make sure we would have pancakes when we got home. It turned out that Saturday morning was pancake and waffle day at the farm. We brought in the gallon jug, and everyone had a feast! Notice God in the details.

Another little detail: I noticed there were only three pumpkins on the porch. I wondered about this since there were four children. As God would have it, I had a small pumpkin packed in the trunk for emergency camp food in case food in the cooler spoiled. That became their fourth pumpkin.

And get this: the first thing the mother did when I told her about the pumpkin in our trunk was to turn to the children and ask, "Did somebody pray?" They had tried to grow plenty of pumpkins, but only got three. When something is orchestrated by God, no detail is left out!

The Fourth Pumpkin

Fun Time

Have events ever lined up in uncanny favor for you? Try asking God to show off on your behalf!

Sky-Hitching

"I had originally planned to get out at Denver even though the plane was going to Salt Lake City, and in fact to Seattle the next day."

So, what is "sky hitching"? Back in 1977, that was an amazing way to get around. You'd just go to a private airport, talk to the pilots there, and if they were going in the direction you wanted to go, you'd ask if you could ride along. It was as simple as that!

I lived in the middle of Ohio, north of Dayton, and I wanted to visit my grandpa who lived in Spokane, Washington. I'd planned to go out there that summer, but I got stuck working at a ministry's headquarters in Ohio.

Here's what I wrote back in 1977:

> *The way God works in our hearts is tremendous. I was planning to go visit Grandpa when I learned that I'd be*

working in Ohio instead. I determined that I should go out to Spokane before the end of October.

That was God telling me, but it took the "manifestation of believing" to get me there. First of all, my department head said no vacations before November 1. Secondly, I didn't have the foggiest idea how I'd get there. Besides, every week was loaded with special occasions, and not only did I see a need for me in the office, I also told myself that leaving was only a trick of the devil.

On the last Monday of October, God screamed in my ear that I should be at my grandfather's on my birthday (October 29). Then there was a hassle in my mind until I decided to talk to an administrator with some clout and share all that was going on in my heart concerning the situation. Every time the weekend came up in my mind, my heart screamed, "You fool, you should be in Spokane!"

I told her that I didn't understand about revelation, but did she think that I should try to go there? (By this time, I had figured out about plane hitching.) She answered by offering to call my department head in Dallas, long distance, and see if she'd give permission. She did, and so did the boss above her.

On top of that, a plane owned by the ministry was being flown to Emporia, Kansas the next day, and I got on it! It just blew my mind how every door opened. Can you see the principles involved here? I finally made up my mind to act, and then doors opened straight through.

When I got to Emporia, I had already decided I should get to Wichita and hitchhike from there. At the Emporia airport, I met a pilot who had just flown up from Wichita to visit his girlfriend, and he came to lunch at our campus and then flew me to Wichita. From there I flew to Denver and then to Salt Lake City over the snow caps in full moonlight. Whoa! I had thought about staying in Denver so I could see the mountains in daylight, but instead, I enjoyed an incredible beauty I'd never imagined.

In Salt Lake City, some guys let me sleep in the executive lounge of one of the small terminals. Earlier that evening, I had been in a larger terminal where the man in charge frowned on sky-hitching. Now at 4 a.m., I was out looking for signs of flight action and went back into the larger terminal to use the bathroom. That was where most of the night planes were landing, and I figured there must be some way I could get on.

I sat down and talked to the clerk, and by 6 a.m. he was convinced he needed to take a Bible class I was promoting, and he helped me get on a flight to Boise, Idaho. I was in Boise no longer than twenty minutes when I met a guy flying to Spokane.

I especially enjoyed this flight because of the pilot's obvious skill. We were in a little two-seater beneath a cloud cover over the mountains, and he knew every peak. As we flew, he explained details about the land formations and pointed out the wild sheep and other wildlife.

It's hard for me to convey how God was with me. Every step of the way I'd have an idea how it would be the next step. Of course, that was revelation, but sometimes it's really hard to accept that, to the point of believing it and acting on it.

For instance, I had originally planned to get out at Denver even though the plane was going to Salt Lake City, and in fact to Seattle the next day. Who knows where it would have led if I had boldly given up the ride to Salt Lake City and remained in Denver? My original *thinking had included a non-stop flight from there to Spokane.*

I knew it was God working in me, and whenever we blow it, He always covers us. The biggest thing I learned was that God will always deliver; there is always a way out; and you will see it as long as you keep your mind aligned with Christ. It's amazing! When you receive no revelation, either you are too bummed out to hear, or there is nothing to do. If you don't know what to do in a situation, chances are it's not yet time to do anything. The place to act is in your mind. Keep putting on God's Word, SIT (speak in tongues), keep your goals straight, and wait. Philippians 4:6 says, "Be careful (old English meaning anxious) for nothing; but in every thing by prayer and supplication with thanksgiving let your requests be made known unto God."

That's my sky-hitching adventure, but I didn't tell you about my visit with my grandfather. It was sweet, and I also got to know my father's two brothers, Tom and Wayne. I recall reiterating to Grandpa about confessing Jesus as Lord and believing God had raised Him from the dead. That's found in Romans 10:9 and has the accompanying promise of salvation. I remember being very bold with my dear grandpa, and I introduced him to some other believers who lived down the street from him.

I loved that trip and have always been thankful that I had such an amazing experience. But why did I have such a burning desire to go in the fall? I knew the ministry I worked for had an event in Seattle scheduled for the following February, and I could have taken our own plane for free all the way to Washington State. I already knew that. Why wouldn't it have been just as good to wait and go see him in February?

My grandfather passed in January. I would have missed him.

Fun Time

When have you ever felt strongly that you should take some sort of action about something, but had no clue why it might be important?

More Sky

"... and all the time I had to keep correcting everything so that the wings were level."

On my birthday, Ron told me to be ready to leave at 4:15 in the afternoon. That's all I knew. But then, about ten minutes before we left home, I asked him if we were going flying. Ron was shocked. All he had said was to bring my camera, but that somehow tipped me off. We met our pilot friend Ed at the airport, and I got to fly up front with him and take over the controls for a while. Basically, I got a very brief pilot's lesson on the fundamentals of flying.

It could have been a lot better if it weren't for the forest fires to the south of us. Visibility was extremely low due to the smoke, and Ed said that we'd land by the instruments when we returned.

I learned that you can't go by your senses if you can't see the ground. In fact, if you can't see the ground, it's almost impossible

NOT to get disoriented. Ed said that if you tried to go by your senses, you could be flying upside down pretty fast. And you'd be moving pretty fast too.

Sounds like life doesn't it? If you try to live by your five senses' knowledge, or worse yet, live by your feelings, you'll find yourself flying upside down in a jiffy. And the more momentum you put behind your error, the worse it gets. We need to understand that God designed man, that He understands how we operate, and let Him have His input. I'm not saying to give God the controls. He has given us both free will and a roadmap. Our job is to use and apply with wisdom what He's put out there.

Ed and His Airplane

When I took the controls of the airplane, I had to watch two of the seemingly ten thousand gauges in front of me. One of them was called an artificial horizon, also known as the altitude indicator, which let me know if the wings were tilted or level. Then there was another one that let me know whether we were ascending or descending.

On our return, directions came in over the air to fly at 4000 feet. We were flying at 5000 feet, so I used the descending/ascending gauge to take the plane down at a certain rate and then kept my eye on another gauge to see when I was getting close to 4000 feet. All the while I had to keep correcting everything so the wings remained level.

Ed loves to teach, and he had me turn left and then back right, showing me how to lower the one wing (which raised the other) and then return them to level. All in all, I had a pretty neat time. Thank you, Ron, for such a fun birthday idea.

Fun Time

Can you think of an experience in your own life where you needed to rely on spiritual knowledge as opposed to natural knowledge?

07

Thumbing to London

"Still, he couldn't drop this foreign lady out on the street just anywhere."

In September 1978, I rode the ministry plane from Dayton, Ohio to Manchester, England for a fun festival. The entire trip was a tremendous series of events and miracles.

We had a few days after the festival to wander as we pleased before the return flight home, which would depart from London. For some reason, I wanted to go to Dublin—I simply believed that God put it on my heart—but I didn't really have enough money to get there and back.

Philippians 2:13 says, "For it is God which worketh in you both to will and to do of his good pleasure." The context of this verse concerns the renewed mind with reverence and obedience to God. When you believe that God is working in you and act on those thoughts (obeying God), then God can work in you. I believed that I was to go to

Dublin, and if God wanted me to go there, then He would have to provide the means to get there.

While I explained my desire to someone, another person overheard me and then took me aside and handed me the cash. WOW!

On the boat from England to Ireland, I met a guy whose family invited me to stay with them. Those two days were wonderful. We even dug genuine Irish potatoes for his mother. She decided to register for our Bible class while I was there and so did a guy I met in the park while gathering chickweed (wild greens) for a salad.

My cash allowance got me back on English shores, but it did not pay for public transportation to London, so I hitchhiked. Everyone in my group was leaving from a particular hotel in London that was a considerable distance from where the boat landed. Our plane was leaving fairly early the next morning, so I was playing it mighty close.

Miraculously, I landed a ride with a gentleman driving all the way to London. It was about 3 a.m. when we entered the city. I had only the name of the hotel, and neither of us had any clue as to where in London it was located. Back then there was no such thing as a GPS.

Cell phones were also still a thing of the future, so nobody in my party knew where I was. They knew only that I was missing; the plane was leaving in a few hours; and they had better pray. I'm sure it was their prayers that prompted that man to stop and pick me up.

At 3 a.m., my driver was not only weary, but also anxious to get home to his family. Still, he couldn't drop this foreign lady out on the street just anywhere. Fortunately, we found a street corner with a policeman, and although he didn't know where the hotel was, he was able to secure me a cab ride to the hotel.

I can still see the joy on the faces of those other girls at the hotel when they saw me. What a relief! (Mary and her wild adventures!)

I believe God sent me to Dublin specifically for that one family to hear His Word.

Fun Time

When have you felt drawn to a stranger, but didn't know why?
Did you dare introduce yourself to that person?

When It Doesn't Work

This is a lesson of thoughts, actions, and reality that God was teaching me on my return trip from Spokane described in Chapter Five. I kept failing at listening to God because my doubt and insecurity kept getting in the way.

"That's the flight I would have been on if I hadn't let that guy convince me there was nothing at that terminal besides military."

Returning from Spokane I blew it royally! First of all, I had decided to leave Wednesday night, and God told me that I wouldn't get to the airport early enough. Sure enough, I took three people to a fellowship, and it wasn't over until after 9:30 p.m.

Old stubborn me, I went to the airport at that hour and got a little bummed out as nothing was flying. I slept on the couch in the women's restroom. At 6 a.m., I decided to go over to a small terminal on the other side of the runway. At that moment I was really trucking. I walked out,, and there was a ride (across the runway) immediately. Then I blew it.

The driver told me there was nothing over there except military, and I believed him. I later found out what a horrible mistake that was. I should have stuck to my decision. I learned that a plane had departed from that airport at 6:30 a.m., and I would have been on it if I had not given in to doubt.

I asked my driver to take me back into Spokane which made no sense at all. Then I asked my Uncle Wayne to drive me to the commercial airport, knowing all along that was a mistake. Then I called another believer to drive me to a private terminal where I was well aware sky-hitching was frowned upon. However, I was back on the right path, and I knew it.

Nobody needed to know I was sky-hitching. I was well-dressed, planted my backpack outside, went in, and sat down ready to get to know any pilot that landed there. It was cool; I even blessed the manager with a compliment on his haircut. I recall hearing in my mind that a plane from Seattle would be landing there, and that it would be the one to carry me the next leg. When asked, I told that to the manager.

Everything was fine. I simply needed to be patient. Then I looked across the runway to the military terminal, and I started to wonder if I should be over there. Damn that doubt. My thought was that a plane would be landing on its way east from Seattle. Why didn't I stand on this as revelation from God? There's no good reason.

My ensuing actions and conversation disclosed the fact that I was sky-hitching, and then the manager made it clear to me that the little military terminal was my ONLY choice. At that point, I hesitantly repeated there was someone coming from Seattle who was to pick me up, and I could see the manager was relenting, but I wasn't strong enough to stick to that as revelation, and I gave in to my doubt.

You ask why I kept doubting after seeing so much success at trusting. That's a good question. Perhaps I had an underlying fear that returning wouldn't be as easy as going. The underlying cause for doubting God's revelation is usually fear.

I returned to the military terminal where it was very loving, and relaxing, but there were no flights going out. Now you get to see why leaving that terminal earlier that morning was a horrible mistake. I sat there and got to greet the men returning from their flight across the mountains to the east! That's the flight I would have been on if I hadn't let that guy convince me there was nothing at that terminal besides military. I'm not making this up. One of those men told me I'd have flown east with them if I'd been there on time. I point this out, not to promote regret, but rather to demonstrate that God had indeed spoken to me.

I sat there the entire day, and knew I needed to wait for further instructions from God. It blows my mind how God was trying to bless me. He sent Christians and others with whom I could relate, and I enjoyed a number of wonderful conversations. However, I would have been farther east if I hadn't allowed fear and doubt to divert me off course earlier that morning.

At the end of the afternoon, I figured I could go back to the private terminal where all the traffic was, as the manager would be gone for the day, and the night guy would probably be more easygoing. That turned out to be God's revelation, because the night manager was super kind. For instance, when he needed to drive out on the runway I got to ride along.

A friend of his was flying to Seattle, and just as that pilot was leaving I had a strong urge to get on his plane even though it was going in the wrong direction. After all, there would be a lot more traffic out of Seattle. I doubted once again, and I didn't get on. He left without me.

That's when things radically changed in my mind. No longer was I receiving any ideas of where or when to catch a free flight east. Instead, my sister Martha in Indiana became very heavy on my heart. That's how God works. I had blown four chances to get across the mountains to the east. First, I didn't get to the terminal early enough the previous night. Second, I believed my driver that only military planes flew from that small terminal. I allowed doubt to cause me to miss an ordained lift across the mountains to the east. My five-senses knowledge stated that there were only military planes flying from that terminal, but the heavenly direction I had received led me there on time. Third, I didn't stick to the revelation that a plane from Seattle would be stopping at the larger private terminal. Fourth, I didn't dare to trust that a flight in the wrong direction to Seattle would set me up for a flight east. Four times I doubted that God was speaking to me.

Now I knew it was God telling me that I needed to get out of there by showing me my sister who lived in Indiana. I borrowed cash and flew commercially to Chicago. Another family member picked me up, and my sister drove me back to where I worked in Ohio.

Jesus warned against doubt:

> *Jesus answered and said unto them, Verily I say unto you, If ye have faith, and doubt not, ye shall not only do this which is done to the fig tree, but also if ye shall say unto this mountain, Be thou removed, and be thou cast into the sea; it shall be done.*
>
> Matthew 21:21

> *For verily I say unto you, That whosoever shall say unto this mountain, Be thou removed, and be thou cast into the sea; and shall not doubt in his heart, but shall believe that those things which he saith shall come to pass; he shall have whatsoever he saith.*
>
> Mark 11:23

Jesus actually reprimanded someone who allowed doubt to enter his mind.

> *And immediately Jesus stretched forth his hand, and caught him, and said unto him, O thou of little faith, wherefore didst thou doubt?*
>
> Matthew 14:31

In Acts, chapter ten, God showed a vision to Peter of non-kosher animals and told him to kill and eat, but Peter doubted it was God. Based on Old Testament Scripture, he "knew" it was wrong, yet it wasn't because God was giving him a different directive. Peter was reasoning with his five senses. Maybe he forgot that Jesus said, "Not that which goeth into the mouth defileth a man; but that which cometh out of the mouth, this defileth a man," (Matthew 15:11). We must judge right and wrong by God's revelation and not be so quick to act according to our natural learning. Human reasoning can be a rip-off if we're not listening to God above.

As I write and revisit my past, I'm reminded of how simple it is to walk with our heavenly Father. We simply learn the Scriptures, and then as long as our thoughts line up with the **values** presented in the Bible, we must dare to believe that God is speaking to us. You can do it also.

Fun Time

Think of or read one of your favorite Scriptures. As you consider the verse, try to be aware of the thoughts you are thinking. Write them down and ask God for His input.

Debbie's Deliverance

"I met her while I was in a hurry to get to fellowship, but God convicted me in my heart to stop and give her a ride."

Debbie Simter brought amazing fulfillment to my life, and as I mentored her, God was radically working with me. I still find it amazing to consider all the revelations I received in order to keep up with her. She was grateful for me as well, but it wasn't like that from the beginning. The following letter from 1990 gives the details.

> I met her while I was in a hurry to get to fellowship, but God convicted me in my heart to stop and give her a ride. So I backed up and took her a few hundred feet to Kroger's, but in that very brief moment, we exchanged addresses and phone numbers. Her name was Debbie Simter. She

had a prevailing hunger for God, and within a few days, she had left a voicemail on our answering machine.

Here's the message. She said that if I were to be her mentor, then I should know some things about her. She explained that she was a homosexual, but that her dream was to get married and raise a child. She also stated that she was a crack addict, an alcoholic, and also (get this) that she ran a ring of girls! Wow!

I knew absolutely <u>nothing</u> about the drug culture, but I was elated to get her message of honesty and willingness to let me be a part of her life, and I immediately gave her a call.

And yes, I was in for a ride. But so was she!
Back to the letter:

Her life has been very rough, to say the least, but it started getting better, just a little bit better, bit by bit. She had successfully refused cocaine for a week, and then messed up and immediately called me at 1:30 a.m. to inform me. I don't remember what I said, but I went back to sleep.

At 3 a.m. I woke up again. That's when she got off work at the bar so I knew it would be closed by the time I got there, but I decided to try to find her anyway. I went looking and almost knocked on her girlfriend's door inside a rooming house. I could hear noises that indicated I might not want to be there, so I left a note under the door assuring her of her righteousness before God.

I was going to drive home, when I decided to at least check if she were at her own place. I remember that free will choice very vividly, because I almost went on home that morning (to return to bed). Anyway, she was home, and that's when God showed off!

I sat down next to her and asked if she'd like to speak in tongues. She said yes, so I explained a little bit about it and how to allow the Holy Spirit to work. She had no trouble at all, and started rattling off in her prayer language! She spoke in tongues—high on cocaine. Wow! How the power of God just cuts through all the junk.

She immediately stood up, and I remember her crying out, 'I stand in awe of the power of God.' Then it was my turn to stand in awe because I didn't have a clue what she was talking about until she continued, "Mary, I've been into drugs for over twenty years, and I know you never come down like this." She was in her right mind, completely sober, shocked, and very thankful. She explained what happens when one starts coming down off the high. That's when the panic stage begins, and the person is willing to do about anything to make the money for the next hit. I was thrilled!

When I left Debbie's place, it was getting on toward 7 or 7:30 a.m., so I went and visited another girl in our fellowship who lived close by, and she was glad to see me because she needed a ride to work. So I got to share with her the exciting news.

God all the way!

I recall another incident with Debbie when Ron and I agreed together to have her stay in our home. Neither of us knew anything about drug users; in fact, it was Debbie herself who asked us if we knew what we were getting in for. She mentioned that there were times she could get violent. But it didn't phase me because I knew for certain that God was behind it.

There were ups and downs, but the ups got higher and the downs became less frequent. I was extremely systematic with Bible study and included her in all my studies. She was eager to learn. I had a three-hour music entertainment video she adored that would occupy her into the late evenings to help her not crave cocaine. She loved gospel music. In fact, she's the one who introduced me to Mahalia Jackson, the singer who traveled with Martin Luther King, Jr.

Here's more from my 1990 letter:

> Debbie has been filling her heart with so much Scripture that she's been growing by leaps and bounds. It's really wonderful spending time with her. She always understands the Word I share or read to her. In fact, I packed my typewriter this morning and brought it over to her place so we could be together.
>
> I left home feeling hard-hearted over a bunch of stuff, but we sat together and read a heap of Old Testament records where the word palal, (the ancient Hebrew word for prayer) is used. What a tremendous time! We came across so many wonderful records of God's deliverance— the Shunamite woman, Hezekiah, Solomon's dedication of the temple, etc. Of course, that was all I needed to get back into fellowship with God, and I came across something that inspired a new goal for my life.
>
> What I want to continue praying for is a perfect heart before God. I thought about what that would do for a person's life. What a powerful walk we can have. If my heart is perfect toward God, then I will _want_ to please Him. Besides, what about that verse in the Old Testament where God said He was looking for people with a perfect heart so that He could show Himself strong for them? Our protection in this spiritual-attack world is guaranteed!

Besides Bible and music, we also had hiking in common and that enabled me to keep her entertained. We spent hours in a nearby state forest with our dog. Lots of times we included some of her nephews.

But there were relapses. One night I remember waking Ron up at 3:30 and saying, "We need to go find Debbie." He believed it was God working in me, so we got dressed, and off we went.

We were well aware of the rooming house where her girlfriend lived, and we drove up only to find Debbie sitting outside on the curb. Just before we showed up, Debbie had said to herself, "It sure would be nice to see Ron and Mary about now," and then immediately, rounding the corner, was our yellow Chevy Malibu. That was a God-moment for her for sure!

Another incident happened inside that rooming house. Debbie was high on something, but I knew that my love for her would pierce through all she was experiencing. The only catch was that I needed to get her to look into my eyes. For her, that was an extremely tense moment. We were closed in a very tiny area at the bottom of the stairway no bigger than 3' x 5'. She acted as if she was trying to take a swing at me, moving her arms and putting on a couple of fierce looks. All the while, I was putting my face into hers and demanding, "Debbie, look at me."

It took some time, but she finally yielded, and our eyes met. It was over; love won the battle. I had no concern for my own safety; I was totally protected by the Spirit of God, and I knew it.

Only one of the tenants in that rooming house could afford a telephone, and he was a rough character. He'd spent a lot of years in prison, and he trusted only a few people with his phone number. Debbie was one of them. I tried to get the number from her so I could reach her there, but she knew better than to share it. One time at our house she caught me watching her dial and quickly stopped, but I got the first five out of the seven digits. (That's before we dialed area codes.)

Then one time I wanted to call her, and figuring she was over at that rooming house, I decided to try every possible combination, using the five digits I knew. That would mean 100 trials from 00 to 99. So

I began dialing: xxxxx00, xxxxx01, xxxxx02, etc. Then I stopped and thought, "If God wants me to call over there, He can give me the two missing numbers."

Right then the digits 4-8 came to my mind. I tried it, and it worked! I doubt that guy ever believed she did not give me those digits, but she knew that God revealed them to me. It was more evidence for her of God's reality. Now over thirty years later, I have no idea what the first five digits were, but I definitely recall those last two!

One time when Debbie and I were out hiking in the woods, the mountain trail took us to a rock where we had an open view across the valley. Debbie sat on the rock, and I stood across from her when she decided that she was ready to be free of homosexuality. We prayed, and I cast that spirit out in the name of Jesus Christ. It was no more than a thirty-second prayer.

I still can see her as she stood up and repeatedly exclaimed, "I feel so free; I feel so free." And she was. But God gives us free will, and she had to refuse to spend time with the girlfriend. Eventually, she returned to some of her old habits.

She lived at our house only for a brief time. Once she felt stronger, she returned to her own apartment. She still attended every fellowship we held at our house, and we allowed her to bring her laundry. One evening after Bible study she was doing her laundry, drunk as a dog. I didn't even realize it, but another woman said, "That girl is drunk."

After everyone else had left, I went up to Debbie and said, "You know we can get rid of this spirit if you want." Her eyes fell and remained glued to the floor as I stood there waiting. Finally, she looked up and said, "Yes that's what I want." Again, a simple fifteen-second prayer handled the situation, and when she got home, she dumped her vodka down the sink. That pretty well ended her addiction issues, and she got a decent job which she kept till the day she died in 2005.

You will recall one of her dreams was to get married and raise a child. She did get pregnant but sadly she chose abortion in order to complete a religious outreach program. She regretted that decision, and I'm sorry to this day that she never fulfilled her original dream. The would-have-been father was engaged to another girl, so who knows how it would have turned out if she had kept the child.

This is also an example of how religion can ruin a life. Having religion and having God are not the same. In many ways, they are complete opposites. God did not create religion. Religion is man-made. God is outside of religion. The Bible declares God, and reading His book enables one to get to know Him. Jesus did not talk about church or a system of beliefs; he talked about a kingdom, which is a governmental body.

In a religious system, there are rules. In a kingdom, people have rights. The Bible is our constitution, and Jesus is our King. The freedom that Jesus brought is found by knowing the truth (John 8:32), and the truth is actually a person, namely, Jesus Himself.

> *And ye shall know the truth, and the truth shall make you free.*
>
> John 8:32

The following is from a poem I wrote to Debbie in 1994:

> *She found a friend, a genuine friend.*
> *Closer to God their lives did blend.*
> *They studied His word and faithful too,*
> *Released door to door and closer grew.*
> *A friendship of God, hearts do melt;*
> *What wonderful moments we have felt.*

Fun Time

Have you ever asked God to reveal some facts to you, facts that would enhance His purpose for someone else?

10

A Love Story

"Later I found out the truth."

By the time I reached adolescence, I was consumed with love topics and guys. My understanding was less than childish, to say the least. As I grew, how to love, what defined love, and such questions often consumed my mind. I met Jesus after a failed marriage, but that didn't mean I automatically understood the truth about love.

During the first couple of years of my born-again experience, I was so excited about Bible knowledge that I didn't give men a whole lot of thought. Gradually my emotional desires rekindled, and I wrote the following story in 1977.

> *A while back I met someone whom I'm really growing to love. He is quite something. A lot of people think he's a real dunce, but that's because they don't really know him.*

Some of my friends got to know him a bit, but they stopped liking him because they never understood him. They said he'd always go back on his word. One girl said he'd promised her a job, but she never got it.

Later I found out the truth. He'd also written her a letter telling her how to go about it, but she never read it. She let someone else read it and relay the information to her, but that person didn't give her the full story.

I wish people wouldn't think poorly of my lover; he's really fantastic. He's always around when I need him and yet he lets me live my own life. He'll give me anything I want unless I get too greedy.

Since I've known him, I've told others what he's really like, and that makes him glad because he wants others to love him too. What blows my mind is that he truly loves me.

Well now, if you capitalize every reference to my lover, you'll have a true story, for my romance is with God Almighty. You can have this same beautiful romance without chasing after someone, because your Lover's love is already established. It's not only neat, it's real! Try falling in love with God.

Fun Time

Have you ever considered God to be your true lover? How would that look in your life?

11

Humor from the Heavenly Comedian

"The next morning I was shocked at what God did."

umor is an interesting topic. Such a title might lead you to think that I'm going to try to make you laugh. But even though you may smile from time to time, and hopefully you do, I'm not trying to be a comedian. I will digress for a second to tell you something I heard from a guy who did claim to be a Christian comedian as well as a prophet. He said that he laughed at his jokes ten minutes before he told them.

I love to laugh, but I must admit it's rare that I get a good hearty laugh out of something I hear from other humans. My husband, Ron's, jokes can be pretty funny, but I've heard them hundreds of times. Thankfully God understands and fills me with such joy that

I don't generally need someone else to amuse me. Just today I was on a Zoom call, and the purpose was inner healing. Inner healing in a group setting is actually fascinating, because the leader has to come up with questions that lead us into connecting with Holy Spirit. In a lot of cases, that means releasing pain, but for me, I just started to laugh. I so enjoy it when Jesus throws laughter my way. I put in the chat that God was raining joy bombs. And He was indeed!

Have you ever noticed how funny God is? His sense of humor is classic. For instance, you've probably read in the Old Testament that, those who seek evil, eventually experience evil coming upon them. And those who seek God and His blessings experience His abundant blessings. So, in the long run everybody gets what they were looking for. God is infinitely clever!

Galatians 5:15 cracks me up. God says, "But if ye bite and devour one another, take heed that ye be not consumed one of another." Think about a bunch of creatures all taking bites out of each other to the extent that they're all consumed. Is this not some of God's clever humor?

Three verses earlier in verse 12 where the context is circumcision, one of the explanations I ran across actually stated, "Let the knife slip." I hadn't realized until then what was implied when God said, "I would they were even cut off which trouble you."

Maybe you could find other examples of God's humor in the Scriptures.

One of the most hilarious times I've had with God happened one cold morning in February, 2007. The previous day, Ron and I had hosted a small gathering where each person gave a twenty-minute scriptural sharing. It was a sweet time, and by 3 p.m. everyone had shared and the party broke up. But Bill and Fran didn't leave. Bill had some points he wanted to make about what I shared. Then he came up with other stuff to talk about, and eventually, I left the discussion to work on a silk worship flag I'd planned to make. Poor Ron was left to deal with Bill, and that didn't go well. Ron also had other plans, but

Bill just wouldn't shut up. Finally, at 6:30 p.m. I somehow offended Bill, and he abruptly summoned Fran and stomped out.

The next morning, I was shocked at what God did. I had my Bible open and pen in hand, planning to journal whatever He laid on my heart. But my thoughts were interrupted with a silly jingle that went like this: "There was this guy I met; obnoxious was his name." I couldn't seem to get that out of my head. It just played over and over: "There was this guy I met; obnoxious was his name." It *had* to be the devil, so I said, "NO" (in really big letters), "God, I want to pray." There it was again. "There was this guy I met; obnoxious was his name." So, I wrote it down. As soon as I did, the following flowed onto the page!

OBNOXIOUS

There was this guy I met;
Obnoxious was his name.
No matter what I said or meant,
His reply was near the same.

An answer always ready,
A dissertation of length,
Such to rob my very life
Of time as well as strength.

Though intent was good at least,
And content full of worth,
The delivery droned on and on:
Of those who'd hear—a dearth.

For _my_ thought or comment
Or occasional full-sentence
Was returned a presentation
Of words without relentence.

Oh if this man could hear
His own voice at times,
Would he alter his reply
Or change the way he chimes?

The one who has the power
Is one who hears a line.
For then he knows the thoughts
That are his and also mine.

Wow! Look at that! Did you know God had that kind of humor? I certainly did not. But there it was. God had seen this situation as obnoxious also. I was simply flabbergasted. But God didn't stop; our redemptive Father turned it into a time of wonderful praise. I was simply jumping up and down in the spirit. Here's the praise that flowed out of me after writing "Obnoxious."

RICH WITH HUMOR

Lord, You are rich with humor.
You can make me smile.
You can give me lightness,
Show me joy for a while.

You are rich with love;
Your humble ways escort me
Into your mind of compassion
Which kindness does support me.

You are easy to be heard;
You speak so very clear.
Your voice is sweet and lovely;
Your lips so very near.

You're the master of my life,
Father of every thought.
The savior of my being
Showing me what I ought.

Lord, stay close beside me;
Never let me go.
Always hold me tightly
So my life will surely flow.

Guide me to my destiny;
Sweep me off my feet.
Then my life will glow
Under the force of Your heat.

You are rich in goodness
And mighty is Your hand.
You are rich in power
Oh, fill this place, our land!

And it didn't stop there. In my journal entries from that day, you will also find jingles including, "If YOU make things happen, I be down here clappin'," or "I'm sitting in a hall of glee, in my day of quality."

And that's where I sit today; I soak in quality from my God. He is mighty and truly, He's everything anyone could possibly need. As He told Moses, "I am that I am." It's been explained that implies He's whoever He needs to be whenever we call upon Him. So, if you need to laugh, be open, and don't be surprised if the God of humor brings you supernatural joy. Let Him give you the time of your life. He is faithful.

Fun Time

Would you like to be able to pick up a pen and paper and simply write things that God is thinking? Try it!

12

The Grizzly Bear

"... if Ron had not thrown that tree as he did, he would have run head-on into that bear ...."

Ron and I were hiking up at a friend's cabin in New Mexico. I sighted a rock on top of a peak that I wanted to reach. We made it in three and a half hours.

Our normal procedure was as follows. We'd start out hiking together, but then I'd get way ahead, so I'd stop and wait for Ron. When he finally showed up, huffing, puffing, and ready for a break, I'd say, "Oh good, now we can proceed!"

At the last slope, he asked me to rest with him a bit, and so I did. But then I moved on up and made it to the top. It was breathtaking in more ways than one. Not only was the scenery scrumptious, but when I got all the way up to my destination rock, I found it to be the edge of a cliff! It was straight down behind me. And

I mean DOWN. Halfway down were the tippy tops of tall pine trees growing way below. And the birds were out there flying at my eye level.

As I sat there taking it all in, Ron started to come into earshot. We were talking back and forth, and since I was above him, I was able to clearly give him a few pointers on which rock to climb first to make his ascent easier.

Now let me reveal something about Ron. There are all kinds of personality tests, and Ron took one that tested reactions. He (correctly) tested to be the type that didn't tend to pick things up. If he perceived an object to be in his way, his tendency would be to step over or around it. I've actually seen him squeeze between a dresser and a dirty sock on the floor to avoid stepping on the sock.

I shared that to explain how Ron's next action was totally out of character. He climbed on a rock where there was a small dead tree lying across it. Instead of stepping over, he actually picked up the tree, heaved it up above his shoulders, and let it drop down behind him, crashing to the ground. It made a huge racket, and my thought was, "Well, I'm sure everybody around heard that!" I did not suspect that we had company.

Ron was coming up from my right, and just at the moment of the crash, movement caught my left eye. I looked and focused my eyes on one enormous rump of a bear before it disappeared behind a rock.

There's no doubt it was a grizzly. It was humongous, and its color was gorgeous, a very rich reddish brown. I then reported in a most non-excited tone that I'd just seen a bear. Ron said, "Yeah, right." Then I said, "Well, actually ...."

Soon we were enjoying our lunch together on that rock, and marveling at how Holy Spirit had been working in both of us. If Ron had not thrown that tree as he did, he would have run head-on into that bear, because the bear had apparently been heading in Ron's direction before turning around. The fact that I spoke so matter-of-factly without the least degree of excitement, I believe, also was inspired by God. God is so amazing, isn't He?

Fun Time

I'll bet there are times when you did something unplanned that really saved the day for you! Can you describe such a time?

God-cidences

"... the Atlanta Ballroom Dance Club had scheduled one of their five annual dances that particular weekend ...."

Many things happen in life in such a way that we consider them coincidences. But why do they happen? And whether they are favorable or not, how many decisions affected the outcome that became the coincidence?

For example, Ron and I went to Atlanta for a weekend event designed to build marriages. The program had some interesting features including a "romantic night out" on Saturday evening. Knowing this; the fact that we like to ballroom dance; and finding out that the Atlanta Ballroom Dance Club had scheduled one of their five annual dances that particular Saturday night caused my heart to soar, to say the least. It was a lovely evening.

Ballroom Dancing

But what went into the decisions of these two completely separate groups to cause that to work out for us so nicely? It was a God-cidence! There have been plenty more.

"Knowing I'd have children showing up in a couple of days, I had to take a look."

I thought I had everything I needed. I was preparing my house for guests—twelve of them, and of all ages. There were five parents, one teenager, and six other children, two of whom were only one year old.

I had created beds where there were none. In one spot I have three trunks standing side by side. I needed another bed in that room, and where the trunks were was a big enough area. But where would I put the trunks? Then the solution came as a sudden inspiration. I laid the trunks on their sides and put a mattress on top—a God-idea indeed.

The office became a bedroom; a breakfast nook became the craft area; and furniture was rearranged. I was ready. Or was I?

Only two days before the first family would arrive, I got a call from my friend Anne, who informed me of a slide, among other things, set out on a curb with a "free" sign. Knowing I'd have children showing up in a couple of days, I had to take a look. What amazing timing!

There on the curb for free were not only a slide, but a toddler-sized three-wheeled scooter and tricycle, a larger tricycle, a small bicycle, a two-seater wagon with the seatbelts intact, and a skateboard trainer. I ended up with all of it.

I thoroughly enjoyed the resulting energy. One baby pushed that scooter all over the dining room. Her three-year-old brother rode that tiny tricycle around and around. I missed a great picture when he passed through the kitchen because my hands were covered in grease as I prepared bacon for breakfast. At a park, the children pulled each other in the wagon.

Look how somebody must have been cleaning out a garage or basement at just the right time for my family's enjoyment. Who engineered that snazzy timing? It was another God-cidence.

"Then the phone rang. It was the security alarm system company."

What prompted Anne to change her mind? Originally, she was going to pick up the medicine for her son and then get gas before she went home. For some reason, she decided to go to the gas station first which positioned her in the car conveniently close to my house. That's when she got my call.

It started out innocently enough. I was in the kitchen, oil in the pan on high flame, onions on the chopping block ready to be thrown into the pan when I saw the text from my friend Jill. She was at Med Express, possibly with a broken ankle.

I dashed out to the car, drove to Med Express, laid hands on her badly swollen ankle and prayed. During the prayer, I felt a strong sense of interaction with God's healing power, but instead of leaving to return home, I decided to remain with her.

Then the phone rang. It was the security alarm system company. Smoke detectors, what's my password, did I want them to call the fire department, etc. It took me a minute, but then I remembered the hot oil in the pan.

I mentally (He reads thoughts) asked God if I needed the fire department and felt peace in my spirit that I did not. I told the alarm company to do nothing, rushed out of there, and got the thought to call Anne. Driving home I dealt with a second call from the alarm people, three red lights, admitting to Ron what was going on, and when I finally got close to home, was relieved to see Anne's car already parked out in front of my house.

The house was full of smoke, but by the time I entered, Anne had things under control with windows opened to air out the place.

And Jill's ankle was not broken.

"Man, I wish I had a boat. I'd sure love to paddle this solo."

I hadn't paddled in a while; I had been living in Kansas where there's no white water, and recently returned to Ohio. There's not much there either, but Ohio is at least much closer to the Alleghenies, where there are lots of fun rivers. One of them is the Youghiogheny, which runs through part of southwestern Pennsylvania before ending at the Monongahela River near Pittsburgh.

At Ohiopyle, the river goes over falls and then actually doubles back on itself 100 feet lower. The "loop" is only a mile long, so a drop like that in such a short distance makes for a lot of thrill. My old canoe club had scheduled their weekend trip there, so I signed up—without a boat!

I called the trip coordinator, Larry, who happened to be someone I'd paddled with in the past, and explained my situation. He said I could ride in the raft that his wife was taking. On that note, I packed my tent and drove to Ohiopyle.

The raft ride was enjoyable, and fairly uneventful, but that old whitewater spirit welled up inside of me as I scouted the waves. It rained that night, and the next morning the river was higher. One girl decided she wasn't going to paddle because she was nervous about the higher water. I asked her if I could borrow her boat. She gave me a reluctant nod, but I could see she was concerned for the safety of her boat, and I was not comfortable taking it.

Then I saw Larry. I said, "Man, I wish I had a boat. I'd sure love to paddle this solo." Without any hesitation whatsoever, Larry replied, "Here, take mine; I'll ride in the raft." WOW. That was amazing. God had me covered.

On the river, as I relayed some of my nervousness due to the fact that I had not paddled in a while, one lady said, "Well, if you get through 'Cucumber' (all the rapids have names), you know you're doing fine." After maneuvering a few more dips and slides, I asked when we were going to get to "Cucumber." The reply was, "You just went through it."

Do you see God in this? A guy who was acquainted with my skills just "happened" to choose the river trip closest to where I lived when it was his turn to lead. And he was the means to reunite me with a sport I'd loved for years.

"Even locating that passport in the first place was suspiciously supernatural."

What about the incident of finding my nine-plus-year-old, still-valid passport? It would expire only one day beyond what was required to obtain a visa to attend a class in India. In other words, if we had applied for that passport only one day sooner ten years ago, I would now need to get a new one.

Even locating that passport in the first place was suspiciously supernatural. Both of us looked through the papers where it should have been and couldn't find it; Ron searched three times. I recalled an incident when my purse had been stolen and imagined the worst.

Then Ron prayed, "God, show us where it is." And, lo and behold, there it was in the papers. Now, how did it get there? Angels? He'd gone through those papers three times already.

Another God-cidence happened in the late 1970s when I set a goal to learn something that would keep me financially stable. Within a week I was assigned to help a dean learn how to operate his programmable typewriter. Little did I know how much I'd need to know about that kind of technology.

Early in 1977 I went out walking among the trailers where I resided. I came across a group of parents who wished they could find someone to tutor their children in math. I had a master's degree in math, and filled the bill.

Another God-cidence occurred when we were required to have unmarked King James Version Bibles for a course we were attending. Within a week, Ron tuned pianos at a church that had just switched to a newer version of the Bible. They were only too happy to give him a couple of their old ones.

Once, when we were planning to leave for a couple of weeks, I needed to find someone to care for my plants. Two days later Ron tuned a piano for someone who loved plants so much she'd constructed a greenhouse in her backyard. She agreed to care for mine, and I was relieved.

And the list goes on—and on, and on and on and on and on and on ....

One could argue that there's nothing to be deduced from these incidents, but there's no point in bothering me with such reasonings. It has happened way too often to convince me that anything besides God Himself is behind decisions that have worked together to bring favor into my life. That's just how He is.

Fun Time

When have you noticed details working out so smoothly for you that it had to be God?

14

Shoppers! Here We Go

"I hid a note in an inconspicuous spot under the fabric lining between the buttons and hung it back on the rack."

I f you didn't know me, you'd swear that this God-cidence is made up. To find the matching top and bottom of an outfit in two different used clothing stores—miles apart—was simply phenomenal, but that's what happened.

Traditionally, the thrift stores I'd grown up with were dark and disorganized, so finding any treasure was rare. Hence, I was pretty excited when I found a store in Dayton where everything was organized by item type, size, color, and even fabric at times. Corduroys had their own section.

Shirts ran half the length of the building in three tiers of racks for small, medium, and large and were even arranged by color. Wow! I could count on finding any top or bottom in a desired color to coordinate with something I already owned. Now that's my kind of shopping! But Dayton was a four-hour drive from home.

Here's what God did. First, I found out this company was a chain, and there were six or seven cities that had one of these stores. Next, He gave me a curious idea. What if I found a friend to take a two-day trip and go from one to the next? What fun that would be!!! It turns out that Ron was the friend, and we started in Columbus.

"... but apparently, no performance at the cash register would convince the sales clerk that I should be an exception."

These stores have a policy that if there's no price tag, they can't sell it. Of course that protects them from accidentally selling something that belongs to another (careless) customer. But for me, this became a real challenge when I found the perfect shirt with no tag.

I really wanted that summer shirt, and once we left Columbus, we wouldn't be returning. The print contained all my favorite colors, but apparently, no performance at the cash register would convince the sales clerk that I should be an exception. Fortunately, I had friends who lived rather close by, so get this. I hid a note in an inconspicuous spot under the fabric lining between the buttons and hung it back on the rack. The note's only purpose was to verify to my friend that she had found the correct garment.

In Akron, I found the bottoms to go with it—the same name brand, fabric, and everything!! Oh man, I had to get that shirt now. I contacted my friend who was able to get to the store, find my shirt—which now had a price tag—and mail it to me. I loved it and bounced around in that outfit all summer long. Thank YOU, Lord!

The Outfit

Fun Time

Waiting for God's solution can be suspenseful. Have you ever had to hang in there before you saw His goodness?

15

The Canine Corner

"The party food was a bag of Purina moist treats for each of them."

One morning, while a friend and I were studying the Scriptures together, she offhandedly remarked that her dog just had puppies. Something leaped in my heart, and I knew I wanted one. Ron had never had a dog before, and I didn't know how the landlord would respond either, but I also knew that whatever had leaped in my heart was supernatural. When God nudges us to do something, He also paves the way for it to be accomplished. When we're open to acknowledge His inspirations, we will experience His intended favor. In this case, everyone agreed, and little Poocher became our first pet.

Tragically, Poocher was killed by a truck before he was three years old. Not long after that, I read of puppies born at a nearby farm and drove out there with a friend. The mother was a golden retriever, and the dad was a black and white mixed collie breed. Some of the puppies were all gold and some were all black. I chose one of the black males and took him home.

His official name was Power, but Pow Pow is what stuck. Before he was old enough to get all his shots, I took him with me to work at someone's home (light garden work), and another guy working there informed me that his dog had just died of parvovirus. This is highly contagious, and just the fact that this guy had walked where his dog had been meant that he was likely carrying it on his boots. Thus, Pow Pow was endangered as well.

Of course I prayed, but little Pow Pow's appetite waned. He was so tiny, and I didn't want to lose him.

I skipped a Bible event one morning, and just lay on our porch with him on my chest as I prayed in tongues. Suddenly, a particular verse of Scripture came to my mind. It was Colossians 1:13, which speaks of us being delivered from the power of darkness. When that verse came to me, somehow, I just knew that Pow would be okay. And sure enough, he began eating, and within a week the vet assured me he was strong enough to get his permanent shots. Yay, God. Thank You so much.

Pow Pow's First Birthday

Pow Pow didn't stay tiny for long. He grew to be 100 pounds. Ron and I loved that dog and enjoyed him for nearly fifteen years. His first birthday was a riot, as you will see, from the following letter dated March, 1992.

Last Wednesday was Pow Pow's first birthday, and I decided to give him a party. I invited four other dogs, but only one of them could come. That was Jams. Jams was often walked near our house, and that's how we met him. He and Pow Pow became friends.

The Bible says, "Whatsoever ye do, do heartily as unto the Lord," and that we did. Jams arrived with his owner carrying a gift bag and card. I had birthday hats for both dogs and, believe it or not, once they got used to them, they forgot about them and left them on for a while.

The party was a great success. Jams' people, Chuck and Ginny, loved the whole concept. As a matter of fact, we won their hearts, and Chuck won mine. He told me that someone had asked him when he was going to make certain phone calls, and he replied that he would do it, but first, he had a birthday party to attend. Then when he explained that the invitation came from a dog, his friend's reply was, "You've really lost it, Chuck." Then Chuck said to me, "People don't know what real fun is." That's what won my heart. Life is to be enjoyed, and the four of us had something in common. We all had love for our pets, and we took that and ran with it. Chuck had his camera, and he ran out of film about the same time I did. It was hilarious.

The party food was a bag of Purina moist treats for each of them. That went well until I tried to get both of them together in a picture. Pow wouldn't budge because he was busy eating his treat. So I moved it over next to Jams, and they promptly fought over it. Ginny reprimanded Jams for not being polite in someone else's yard. I was laughing so hard I didn't try very hard to separate them.

I saved the party favor rawhides until Jams was ready to leave.

A poem written by one of Pow Pow's stuffed animal toys.

Dirty and gray has become my plight.
Before, I was beautiful, fluffy, and white.
I'm Pow's gorilla
No longer vanilla,
I'm slimy or grimy all day and night.

I'm there for Pow—in joy or pain;
His fill of me is my life's gain.
I have no eyes,
Nor am I wise
'Cause long ago he gutted my brain.

Sometimes I lie in middle of floor;
Am I forgotten? Am I a bore?
Then comes Pow
After his chow,
And grunts and chews and gnaws once more.

His teeth are white as I once was
His fur is striking; I'm barely fuzz.
My guts are missing;
Others are hissing—
Soon I'll be the ape that was!

Years later Power died of old age, and we were dogless for a little over a year. At first, we really enjoyed the freedom of being able to easily go where pets weren't allowed, but that changed.

I noticed an apathy towards normal home life that was not natural for me. Whenever Ron came home from work, however, suddenly I was motivated to get everything done that I had avoided during the day. When I explained this new development to Ron, he realized that I needed companionship and proclaimed we should get another dog.

Finding a dog was not as easy as it had been in the past. People no longer put ads in the town newspaper when they had unwanted puppies. I didn't want to go through the trouble of pet adoption, so I prayed for God to put a dog in my lap.

One day, when I was at the back of our property, I noticed that a neighbor had a new cute puppy, and I inquired where she got it. I tried calling the number she gave me, but nobody ever returned my call. After a month or so, the neighbor called me to explain that they were not going to keep their puppy and asked if I wanted it.

Instead of taking the puppy, we worked it out that I would help housebreak it, so it would be easier for them to keep the dog. That idea only lasted two days when my neighbor called again to say her uncle was going to build a doghouse, and they planned to keep the dog tied outdoors.

The doghouse never appeared, and after another month, she called again to see if I wanted the dog. It was a female border collie mix named Shiloh. At this point, Ron and I agreed to pray about it.

In the meantime, I was learning to use writing as a way to spend time with God. I'd pick up my journal and write a prayer or praise, and before I finished the paragraph, I would notice much of it was inspired. On this particular morning, I picked up my journal, expecting to write sweetness from God. What appeared on the page, however, was the following: "How much in your lap do you want?" I recalled my original prayer of asking for a dog to be put in my lap and realized this was God's answer. I walked back to the neighbor's house, and Shiloh became my new canine friend.

Shiloh had one of the sweetest dispositions I've ever encountered in a dog. Ron used to say she was the "sweetest sweet sweet of the sweets that ever sweeted." In spite of her sweetness, some dogs could trigger a completely different persona in her, but she was always kind to people, including children.

I had her highly trained and you can watch her on YouTube if you search for shilohshishi*. Please note: the asterisk is part of the address to search for. Google will ask you if you meant something else, but you have to stand your ground if you'd like to watch Shiloh climbing down ladders backward, or bringing my towel to the bathtub, or racing up two flights of stairs to the third floor to fetch my car keys while I'm waiting on the first floor.

I used to take her to a local nursing home where she, Ron, and I would put on a forty-five-minute show. She also performed at birthday parties. Videos of her practicing are on YouTube as well. Kids loved her, and she brought joy everywhere we went. Apparently, God even cares about our pets. He certainly made sure I got an amazing companion.

Fun Time

Do you have any pets? Have you prayed for them?

16

Two Miracles in One

"Meanwhile, two floors up in the prayer room, Leslie heard my first yelp as she was in the middle of praying that she be where the Lord wanted her to be at that moment."

Sometimes God accomplishes His work by having someone in the right place at the right time, and such was the case on Wednesday, November 15, 2006.

A friend of mine, Leslie, stopped by, and since we have a prayer room on the third floor of our house, she decided to take advantage of it and spend a few minutes in prayer in that room.

I decided to check out a latch on some newly installed storm windows on the first floor. The original double-hung window set was still intact. I knew that both ropes connecting the upper window to the window weights were broken, and in order to avoid having it come crashing down unexpectedly, I had asked the window installer to cut a piece of wood the right length to hold up the top window, and I watched him put it in there. Hence, I unlocked the sash lock, confidently grabbed the top of the lower window to lift it up, and OUCH!!

The upper window came crashing down, and the top of it grabbed my fingers in such a way that not only was I experiencing pain, but I quickly realized I was ensnared by the window. Someone had taken the piece of wood out and not put it back.

Meanwhile, two floors up in the prayer room, Leslie heard my first yelp as she was in the middle of praying that she be where the Lord wanted her to be at that moment. Well, she was—although it didn't have anything to do with the original reason she was speaking that prayer.

She heard me holler, "Leslie, come down here!" She was already at the doorway, and made it down to me in a flash.

Both of us, with my one free hand and her two, tried with all our might to lift that top window to no avail. We then tried to separate the two pieces of wood horizontally, but no success. You might wonder why it would be such a problem to simply raise the upper window. The answer lies in the old construction of double-hung windows. When the upper window is lowered all the way, the two frames lock together in such a way that the process of raising it pulls the wood together more tightly. That's what was trapping my fingers.

The entire time, we were calling out to the Lord (loudly) to get the window up, to set my fingers free, to continue the circulation in my fingertips, etc.

I sent Leslie for the claw hammer, but we couldn't manage to insert the claw where it needed to go. I then realized we needed the crowbars, but I knew I'd have to explain to Leslie how to find them in the basement.

Next, the phone rang. Leslie held the phone to my ear while I used my free hand to ease the pressure slightly. Some lady wanted to know who I was since our number had appeared on her phone bill. I asked her if she was a Christian, and she said, "No." I told her I'd be glad to speak with her later, but right then I needed someone to pray for me; my fingers were stuck between two windows. She hung up (and never called back), and I proceeded to give directions for the crowbars.

Leslie reported that when she got to the basement, she had no idea which direction to go, so she asked the Lord. He pointed her to the left, and she found the crowbars. It seemed to me she was back in no time. We successfully raised the window, and as it started up, it actually pinched my fingers harder.

It was then that I realized my fingers were actually holding the window down.

Having already experienced the miracle of Leslie being there to help free me, I felt my healing was inevitable. I had no doubt that my fingers would be completely restored. In fact, three hours later I played the duet part with one of my piano students and actually forgot I'd had a problem. My fingers were perfectly fine.

It's glorious! My fingers were healed. But as I see it, the main miracle was that somebody else was in my house! I was trapped at the window with no way to escape. There was no phone within reach, and to open the outside (storm) window to shout at someone happening by also was impossible since the latch was at the bottom of that window and blocked by the two windows trapping me. It occurred before 1 p.m., and Ron didn't return home that afternoon until after 5:30 p.m. I'd have been trapped there for four and one-half hours if Leslie hadn't been present.

Oh, the magnificence of our God to have someone there for me!

Fun Time

Did you know you can expect God to heal you of ailments, aches, and pains? Lay your hand where you're experiencing a problem and command your affliction to leave you alone.

17

Camping in Three Feet of Snow

"In other words, if we met a vehicle on the road, somebody would have to back up a mighty long way."

One November, Ron and I set dates for a winter backpack trip. We felt assured that we would not have any precipitation, since on a previous trip with our outing club, we'd had enough for the entire season. About five days before the trip, Ron mentioned Otter Creek to our friend, Dwayne, on the phone, who promptly exclaimed it was buried in two feet of snow. He tried unsuccessfully to suggest alternate trails. Well, Dwayne, you were wrong. There was three to five feet of snow, depending on where you put your feet!

We found the road down to the trailhead. Was it passable? We weren't sure as we did not have a four-wheel drive vehicle. As we were debating whether to park on the highway, a truck came out, and the driver said it would be drivable for a car, but there was NO passing room. In other words, if we met a vehicle on the road, somebody would have to back up a mighty long way.

We had a quick word of prayer and then proceeded. We made it to the parking area. There were a few hunters there waiting for the season to open. They had intended to pack in, but all that snow convinced them to set up camp next to their vehicles.

While we wasted precious daylight hours, a couple of other pickup trucks arrived at the trailhead. I noticed one of them leave, and then about five to seven minutes later, he returned—backward followed by the vehicle driving forward to the trailhead. I thanked God that we didn't end up in that predicament.

Finally, we got serious about moving on, and boy, were we grateful for Dwayne's warning. Because of his report, we'd abandoned the idea of hiking boots and purchased waterproof, felt-lined boots the night before. They were what enabled this trip to be a lighthearted, fun-filled time. Thank You, God, for having us call Dwayne before we made the trip.

The boots first proved their worth when we arrived at the stream, with virgin snow on the footbridge deep enough to reach way up to the handrail. We walked through the shallow water instead.

Once on the trail, we needed to find a campsite right away because our daylight was very limited. There was one place where the trail seemed to split: one part, straight ahead, and the other, on an easy incline. I had no idea which was our intended trail, but we chose the upper. It probably was an old forest road. Anyway, there was plenty of room for a tent and a fire up the way.

I had the idea, since the snow was at a perfect packing temperature, to roll snowballs to clear the area. It was a great idea, but there wasn't time. Wouldn't that have been snazzy to have a great big old snowman there on the trail to entertain the hunters?

Anyway, once we figured out that a fire on the upside of the trail might melt the snow above to put the fire out, I placed our twigs over to the other side. I had newspaper for fire starter, and we barely had enough time to gather what I thought would be enough wood for the evening. We lit one match, and the fire would almost go out, and then start up again. When I informed Ron that if the fire didn't go, we could eat power bars, and forego the beef stroganoff, he got seriously interested in the fire. With another word of prayer and some serious blowing, the fire miraculously took off like crazy. I had saved enough newspaper for the morning, and we still hadn't needed to light the second match. The beef stroganoff was delicious. The snow was deep enough that when we sat on it, it was packed high enough to be our seats. Our feet were on the clear ground below next to the fire.

Sunday morning, I gathered some wood and then threw some newspaper on the white ashes. To my amazement, the paper immediately started smoking! By the time I got the sticks laid up, it burst into flames. Breakfast (at noon) was hash browns, onions, ham, bacon, and eggs. We cooked the whole weekend in the snow, using only one match!

In the afternoon, we climbed the steep slope to the top. Our black retriever dog, Pow Pow, was frustrated at times because he couldn't take the lead in some of the snow drifts. So, he'd fall behind in my footsteps. It was slow going, lots of fun, and great exercise. At the top, it was cold enough to lie back in the snow side by side without getting wet. We really enjoyed looking up at the clear blue sky and sunlit treetops—that is until Pow Pow ran up to us and shook snow all over our faces.

Afterward, we walked all the way down to the creek before returning to break camp. We found that rhododendron thickets are easier to navigate in heavy snow than in the springtime, because you can literally walk over the top of them. The snow had caught most of the leaves and buried them so the trunks were all leaning over. We simply walked over the top with one minor challenge. You never knew if you'd be stepping down one foot onto a branch, or three or four feet down to the ground below.

The stream was gorgeous, and so was the entire weekend. All of it is evidence of God's beauty and infinite variety.

Fun Time

Do you ever rave about a sunset or lovely hillside? Try thanking God for His infinite artwork.

18

Finding Site Number Forty-Two

"I awoke a third time, but before I finished deciding whether to get out of bed, I was waking up a fourth time under a shining sun with a cloud cover moving in."

Ron dropped me off one evening at a state park near where he would be attending a conference. I would be embarking on a two-day camping/prayer vigil in approximately three feet of snow. I was one of a party of three: me, my 100-pound dog Pow Pow, and the Lord. It was a precious time.

There had just been a huge snowstorm in the area, and the year-round campground was only plowed to site #1. I had called ahead and already knew what to expect, so I had my gear packed in a backpack plus an extra bag with skids so Ron would be able to pull it across the snow for me.

When we arrived at the entrance where there was a layout map of the campground, I picked out site #42. I had looked at different possibilities, but #42 seemed like the one I was supposed to find. That's how God works. Then off we trudged (after dark) by the light of the crescent moon to find roads and marked posts. Every picnic table looked like a snow-covered car, the gap between the tabletop and seat being the windows.

We went way past where the turn-off to #42 should have been, so we put our stuff down, and I was able to scout a bit more easily. I never saw the road, but I did find a clearing that looked like it was in the direction of where the site should be, so I ventured out across the glade. Down one hill, over a small snow-covered stream, and up the other side, and lo and behold, there was a picnic table. I found the beginning of the drive to discover it was #39, and I knew I was getting close. Then I trudged just a bit further and found a table in a really neat-looking spot. I very much liked the way it looked. The layout had a level area next to a steep downward slope. The table was on the other side of the level spot, and trees circled around. Then I went to the post to see what site it was. You guessed it; it was #42. Home!

Ron was a good sport through the whole ordeal, and Pow Pow was ecstatic. I was glad to have found a non-road entrance to my spot, because that meant there were no traces on the road leading to my camp. I preferred complete privacy. When I went back to the car to see Ron off and get the phone number of his motel, a ranger drove up. He asked if we were going to camp, and I said, "Yes." He said I'd better have my snow shoes, and I showed him my boots. After I told him I'd already spoken with reservations the day before, he drove off. Since Ron left with our vehicle, I suspect that he figured we gave up and decided not to camp. That was fine with me for the time being.

I didn't use the tent that first night, but put a light down bag inside an old rag poly-filled cotton bag on top of an old tarp. I also had an insulation pad under my down bag inside the cotton bag. One extremely critical detail in winter camping is to have adequate protection from underneath. It's the ground first, not the air, that steals body heat.

It was a gorgeous clear night with only a small bit of black sky between all the stars! Spectacular!

I guess God wanted me to enjoy those stars because I woke up three times. In fact, the night turned into quite an ordeal. The first time I awoke, I knew I needed to get all the way up because I was slightly cold. It's not a good idea to get cold in that kind of weather. I considered going to the lodge to see about borrowing a wool blanket to put under me. I already had my wool pants and sweater under my body on top of our best insulation pad, so I was mildly surprised. That's before I figured out that water somehow was getting up to me from underneath. Anyway, I hadn't figured all that out when I got dressed and took off for a prayer walk in hopes of finding the lodge.

This turned into a two-hour walk that involved finding a map of the park, where I learned I'd only made it halfway to a lodge. How badly did I need to borrow a blanket? Not bad enough. I returned to my camp and discovered the wet bag. Fortunately, I came with lots of plastic and several tarps because I had planned for melting snow. "Thank You, Lord, for helping me pack."

I put one small tarp between the cotton bag and the pad under my down bag. I also remembered that there was another wool sweater in my complete-change-of-clothes bag and got that for under my head. Then back to sleep.

I woke up another time and walked to the payphone in the middle of the campground to check our home messages. Then I took another prayer walk before returning to finish my sleep.

I awoke a third time, but before I finished deciding whether to get out of bed, I was waking up a fourth time under a shining sun with a cloud cover moving in.

That morning, I put up a clothesline, and the cotton bag was dry by evening. I heated water with charcoal in a small table-top cooker, cleared the snow from the table so it would finish drying off, and then embarked on my day with the Lord. I'd find a place to pray for a while, and then when the cold started to permeate through my layers, I'd walk on and find another spot. The hiking was great, and in my reflection time I wrote two poems. At one point, when Pow Pow was checking out a different direction, fifteen to twenty deer crossed the valley in front of me. More than likely, they were escaping from the dog.

Upon return to camp, I knew I was in for a treat—collecting standing dead trees for wood, dragging them up that steep incline to camp, building a huge fire, and cooking up a Cajun rice mix. This might seem weird to some, but I love this kind of work. I had a rip-roaring fire going in no time with plenty of extra wood, and the food was delicious.

The second night, I stuck an extra piece of plastic over the tarp where my body would be, then put the tent on top of that and moved inside. Pow was shivering, and so I let him inside the tent. He started on the upside of me and almost shoved me out of bed, so I coaxed him to the other side. He continued to shiver, so I ended up sharing a section of my pad with him.

At one point, I woke up and took a prayer walk. It could have been early morning hours; I'm not sure. But once again, I felt God's timing. He knew it was going to sleet, and I was already safely back in the tent before it started! However, I got back up and spread my last big tarp across my tent, ground tarp and all, anchoring it with wood.

Another cool fact was what I discovered had happened in the campground during that day. Two of the three camp circles had been plowed out, but naturally, I was in the one closed area, my privacy preference still being honored. I say "naturally," because that's how God works. Why did I have the idea of staying in site #42 in the first place? I hadn't been there before; it was just one of those nudges from

God. He knew the other roads would get plowed out before I left, and He was privy to my desire to remain private.

By morning it was above freezing, and there was a continuous drizzle the entire day. The fireplace and wood were completely soaked. I took that tarp from over the tent and erected it above the table, using my leftover trees from the burn pile as poles. Again, I was thankful for how I'd packed. God will inspire our actions when we acknowledge Him.

The tarp was plenty high to safely cook with my charcoal burner on top of the table. I heated some water and then abandoned camp for another prayer walk. By this time Pow was ready to hang close to me and not run around so much. He was tired, and the wet snow wasn't comfortable for him.

I could have thrown some sticks for him, but I didn't give him much attention. When we returned to camp, he walked straight into the tent and plopped himself right on top of my bed, right in the middle. The look he gave me was, "Now, it's my turn!"

I read from *The Message* New Testament, cooked some cream of leek soup, most of which I gave to Pow Pow to warm him, and then it was time to pack up and leave.

When it was time for Ron to show up, I was getting ready to go to the road to flag someone to send a ranger my way so I could pay for the site. Just at that moment, a ranger drove in! God is so cool!

Fun Time

Sometimes we keep going and learn that God has a prize waiting for us. Can you think of an experience where that happened to you?

19

Quizzical Cuisine

God opens multiple doors for us and often gives us the choice of which ones to walk through. In this chapter, you will learn of a huge door that I did not enter. I will never know what my life would have been like if I'd gone in that direction, but God never abandoned me. He just took the route that I chose. He'll do that for you too. So even if you mess up, He's still there to pick you up.

It's impossible to mess up so badly that you cannot turn to God for help. Consider how David in the Bible killed a wonderful godly man after taking his wife. Yet God picked up the pieces, and David went on to more greatness.

The apostle Paul was out looking for Christians in order to have them imprisoned, if not put to death, and he ended up being a mighty man for God. He even is the one who got the revelation to write many of the epistles of the New Testament.

So you see, God can turn lemons into lemonade.

"At some point Jack suggested we be the founding members of 'The Gluttons Club,' and since I always ate so much, he decided I should be awarded the golden pig."

Depending on your viewpoint, my first husband, Oz, and I shared either the delights or horrors of exploring food combinations. Our guests were well aware that coming to our place for dinner would be an adventure, to say the least. My mother, for one, was never sure if it would be safe or not. My sister, Martha, on the other hand, always anticipated fun delights.

One couple in particular, Jack and Angie, absolutely adored our cuisine boldness, and they were not afraid to come up with some of their own as well. Often, we would invite them for dinner or be invited to their place. The four of us engaged in an unwritten competition to see who could come up with the wildest menu. At some point, Jack suggested we be the founding members of "The Gluttons Club," and since I always ate so much, he decided I should be awarded the golden pig.

I remember one time Oz and I decided to put on an eleven-course Chinese banquet. As I recall, we had thirty-six people present. We wanted to be sure that everyone had a chance to try everything, so we portioned out each course in extremely small amounts. For instance, we prepared eighteen egg rolls for one course, and each guest received half an egg roll.

You would have thought these people had been starved for months the way they complained about getting such a tiny amount—until they reached somewhere between the sixth and eighth course. Somehow, the sentiment changed entirely.

Oz and I had planned very carefully and worked extremely hard to make sure every ingredient of each combination to be served was numbered accordingly. Since the Chinese end their meals with something light such as fresh fruit, we served the ten precious pudding next to last. This is the dish that later brought me some fame.

It's a sweetened rice pudding loaded with dried fruits and layered in the middle with a rich date paste. The entire pudding is steamed in a bowl lined with fruit laid out in an inviting arrangement and then served by turning it upside down onto a platter. One must carefully lift the bowl so the design remains intact for full view.

After everyone had oohed and aahed over the masterpiece in front of them, they all dug in. I assure you there were remarks like, "I don't have any more room, but I have to try this." Needless to say, we had lots of fresh fruit from course number eleven remaining for the next day.

After Oz and I broke up, I took my talent to the street. I befriended a couple who owned a shop on Main Street and set up my wood-burning stove on the sidewalk in front of their place. There I sold my version of "pork paos," (soft and fluffy steamed buns with a pork filling). Not only did I make some cash, but I also drew customers into their store—and it was a lot of fun.

In 1975, my life took a glorious turn. I confessed Jesus Christ as my Lord and Savior and believed in my heart that God had raised Him from the dead. My reasoning was that if God can create man in the first place, surely He could raise one from the dead.

I paused my cooking escapades, took off with my newfound interest, and intensely pursued Bible knowledge exclusively for the next four years. Then, in the fall of 1979, I moved to Jonesboro, Arkansas, where I again began to display my cooking abilities. God was with me all the way. Looking back I can see how He was opening doors for a catering-type business. First of all, the local newspaper wrote up

TAKING TO THE STREET IN A UNIQUE WAY is Mary Wehmanen, who was selling "Pork Pows" in front of Grapevine, Albion's newest restaurant, on South Superior Street, during the Albion Sidewalk Days Friday. Ms. Wehmanen said that item was her own special recipe, made of oriental steam bread with pork stuffing, covered with a special sauce. She was cooking on a wood-fired stove.
(Recorder Photo)

Cooking on the Street in Albion, Michigan

a very nice article with a great picture of me revealing a precious rice pudding. That's the same recipe I used for my eleven-course Chinese dinner party.

Opens Catering Business—

CATERER MARY WEHMANEN
Unmolding A Precious Rice Pudding

I also had the newspaper article from the street cooking I had done, as well as a few letters of recommendation. It was wonderful advertising to have statements such as the following: "Her menus are creative and original, and what is more, she seems to have a love for cooking."

With this free promotion, it was simple to begin a very nice business. Since I was not interested in complying with various laws of owning a restaurant, I simply hired myself out as a private cook for one night only. Calls came in immediately from women who wanted an interesting meal for their dinner party, and the game was on—except for the confines of religion.

I was still very involved with a Christian ministry, and we had meetings close to four or five times per week in the evening. Dinner parties happen in the evening. Something had to give, so I gave up the dinner parties. Looking back, it's obvious how God had been promoting me, and I now believe I could have been part of bringing wealth back into the kingdom of God had I pursued the dinner party career.

I don't regret my decision to grow with God, and He never lets us drop. My life has always been rich with blessings and delights (not all of which were edible.)

Furthermore, my husband Ron loves crazy food! It's another God-cidence.

Fun Time

What choices do you have? You can ask God to show you the best route knowing He'll stick with you as long as you acknowledge Him.

A Sister Indeed

"Since I was bound to finish a letter to her, I asked her what I should write."

Martha had not written in a long time. I was going to summer school at UCLA Berkeley and decided I was going to make a strong case for her to write to me. So I wrote a very terse letter: "Dear Martha, WRITE! Love, Mary." Did it work? It did! In no time at all I was excitedly opening an envelope from her. "Dear Mary, OK. Love, Martha."

And then there was the time when I was new to the computer world and decided to learn Word Perfect. I had just typed, "Dear Martha," when the phone rang. It was Martha. Since I was bound to finish a letter to her, I asked her what I should write. She told me that she would like me to send some directional Scriptures. So I did. Here are a few of them.

Dear Martha,

Deuteronomy 3:27 - Get thee up into the top of Pisgah, and lift up thine eyes westward, and northward, and southward, and eastward, and behold it with thine eyes, for thou shalt not go over the Jordan.

Acts 22:10 - Arise, and go into Damascus, and there it shall be told thee of all things which are appointed for thee to do.

Genesis 22:4 - Make me savory meat, such as I love, and bring it to me that I may eat.

Love,
Mary

Martha and Mary

Martha had an amazing sense of humor, and often we would make up silly poems back and forth.

So, what does this have to do with God? Everything. God loves humor; He loves clever expressions; He loves adventure. Most of all,

God loves to see His children joyous. God is always willing to accompany us wherever we go, in whatever direction we choose. But we're the ones who choose to take Him with us. When we give credence to His presence, He adds to the fun. He gives me ideas when I'm looking for something clever to say. If I want something humorous, He fills in the blanks. He did it continually with both Martha and myself.

Fun Time

Have you ever gotten interesting ideas that turned out to be really fun? Consider that God was inserting them into your mind.

21

April Fools

22

April Fools Explained

"As she paused to read each sign, the suspense mounted, ..."

April Fools should be fun, but some people have turned it into a day to tell lies. In fact, for some, anything goes. Sadly, one mother was told her son was in a serious car accident, and after nearly having a heart attack, she learned it was only a joke. That's not a joke.

So what about April Fools? God doesn't need it for His people to have fun and enjoy life. But God is in favor of His people enjoying life, and I will be the first to admit that I've spent time and gone out of my way to play some of the jokes I'm about to describe.

Once, I switched the contents of two cupboards in Debbie's kitchen. This is the Debbie Simter you read about in chapter nine. When she went to fix her breakfast on April 1, the bowls and cereal were backward. She told me she laughed hysterically.

Ron and I performed at a nursing home on April 1, 2006. I held my flute and wore a sign that read "Concerto Grande." Ron sat at the piano with his back to the little ladies, and wore a sign that read, "For Piano and Flute." Then we both put on a silent show, complete with swaying and elaborate movements to the imagined music. After thirty seconds or so, I turned over Ron's sign which then read, "April Fools." The ladies loved it.

Why not have some fun? Better yet, why not ask God for an idea? He has an infinite supply.

Here's one I came up with after inviting God into my game. Debbie was staying at our house, and I wanted something unique for when she returned from work in the evening.

Instead of figuring out a practical joke, why not simply make her think there would be one when there really wasn't? I accomplished this with a series of signs she would see on her way to her bed.

Every sign was a Scripture that assured her not to be afraid. Of course, after reading them, she would think there would be a scary situation awaiting her. The signs were simple enough. For instance, one was 2 Timothy 1:7 "For God has not given us the spirit of fear, but of power, love, and a sound mind." Another was Acts 18:9 "Then spake the Lord to Paul in the night by a vision, Be not afraid ..." and so on.

As she paused to read each sign, the suspense mounted, and she was somewhat apprehensive about what she might encounter before reaching her bed. When she finally arrived, there on her pillow was a sign that simply read "April Fools." She loved it.

In 2019, my friend, Anne, brought a most delicious cake to my April first dinner party. What "takes the cake" is that she presented it in a cat litter container with a purple scooper as the cake server. And to top it off, she decorated it with turd-shaped brownies. She even glazed them with a clear syrup so they appeared to be fresh poop. Of course, it was hilarious.

One guest, not realizing what she was actually saying remarked,

"These are the best-tasting turds I ever ate." Another guest joked, "You've heard of Duncan Hines; well, now you've heard of Puss 'n Boots."

Even in mischief, God can be included. Let Him be in all your life, not just part of it. Watch how much fun He can be. You don't need to wait until the next April 1.

Cake for April Fools' Day

Fun Time

Can you figure out how to make someone believe a joke you're pulling without telling an actual lie?

Who Got the Job?

"Steve was the manager, and he said, 'You know, I can't just hire off the street.'"

Who got the job—me or God? My heart simply swells over all the times God has been my assistant, my spokesman, and my encourager.

I arrived in Jonesboro, Arkansas in August of 1979 without a dime to my name. That's because I had done something stupid on the way, which resulted in my purse being stolen. It contained a $100 bill, a gift. I had just graduated from a Christian ministry's leadership training program, and Jonesboro was my first assignment. Fortunately, I had a contact with whom I could touch base. They welcomed me into their modest home and would have gladly helped me more if they'd been aware of my plight. I was too ashamed to tell them. Maybe there was a bit of pride on my part, but that couple was not flowing in cash, and God was my sustenance.

I went to the labor-for-a-day place and had no trouble finding work as well as winning the hearts of several employers. Within a couple of weeks, I secured a reasonable house by convincing the owner of a couple of things. First, he allowed me to pay the security deposit in monthly installments of $25 each. (Life was a lot cheaper back then.)

Second, he agreed to leave the electricity in his name until the end of the month. The month ended on a Friday, and I had $60.29 to my name. My understanding was that the electric deposit was $30, so my plan was to switch it to my name and then go job hunting. The remaining $30.29 would easily get me through the weekend. When I arrived at the electric company, I was informed that the deposit was $60, not $30. Oops. I plunged downward in my mind and left the building.

I was traveling by bicycle at the time, and there was a nearby house where a couple of guys lived whom I knew from my ministry involvement, so I rode over there. That's where the battle took place. I mean that was the physical location of my body while the battle took place in my mind. I'll call the two views Alice and Wonder.

Alice: If I pay the $60, that will leave me with only 29 cents for the weekend and no job.

Wonder: You have to pay the deposit if you want electricity.

Alice: How in the heck can I live with only 29 cents for the entire weekend?

Wonder: You know God promises to meet every need (Philippians 4:19). You have the $60!!

Alice: Ooooh, this is scary. I thought I'd have $30 left over.

Wonder: You know Jesus said He came to give you life and that it be abundant (John 10:10).

Alice: I don't think living without electricity is an abundant life.

Wonder: You have the $60. Go pay it.

Alice: I'm not sure about facing the weekend with only 29 cents. But it's true what you're saying.

Believe it or not, this conversation went on in my mind for an hour. Then I hopped on my bike, rode to the electric company, forked over the $60, and rode across town to follow a job lead at a salad bar at Western Sizzlin restaurant.

Steve was the manager, and he said, "You know, I can't just hire off the street."

"Yeah, I know. I'll work today on trial. If you like my work, then you can hire me at the end of the day."

Steve agreed, and I'm a great worker, so at the end of the day, he awarded me the job. Since I had not yet officially been put on any payroll, he went over to the cash register, pulled out $24, and gave me my day's wages!

So I had electricity, cash for the weekend, and a full-time job. The victory was in that I made my decisions that morning as a result of what the Bible teaches.

The Alice and Wonder conversation shows how I had to make up my mind that what God wrote was trustworthy. I had to submit and trust that He meant what He said: that He wanted abundance for me, and that He would meet all my needs. I got both.

So who got the job—me or God? I did the work, and He did His work in the hearts of people, which, in this case, resulted in my employment and security.

Fun Time

When have you had a battle in your mind similar to the Alice and Wonder conversation? Who won? Did the final outcome line up with Scripture?

24

Everything Goes Right

"But then one day I noticed something I'd never seen before."

Have you ever tried to describe the details of your day? Do people listen to you? I've seen conversations between two women who both were excitedly sharing, but neither one had the least idea what the other was talking about.

I also have caught myself giving too much detail and boring my listeners. Does God do that? If you're familiar with the Bible, you know there are whole chapters that relate who gave birth to whom. In 1 Chronicles, the first nine chapters are nothing but that. That entire section of Scripture is about so and so begetting so and so, and it goes on and on. Who would want to read that?

But then one day I noticed something I'd never seen before. Not only did the verses say who begat whom, but every now and then a detail was thrown in about somebody being the one who did such and such.

Suddenly it dawned on me that God was just talking about His kids. Do you know how two people who haven't seen each other for a long time talk? They usually catch each other up on what happened with this child and with that one, who married whom, and other details of family and friends.

What about God? I guess He made us to be like Him, so wouldn't it make sense that He'd just want to catch us up on His kids? When I realized the love in those nine chapters, the details took on an entirely new character.

So I'm going to take a chance and give you the details of one particular day. Please be assured that in the detail is the amazing element of God blessing this particular kid. He seems to make a regular practice of it.

"I didn't have a lot of cash on me, but I needed a few things at Kroger's and didn't want to stop by home first."

It was 1992, and I was so elated with how the day went, I decided to put it in writing.

We all talk about the big things that happen in life, but we all know it's the little things that really make it sing. I'm going to share all those little things that made one particular day a big thing.

I woke up that morning with a few chores on my mind. I hopped out of bed and did them: changed the sheets, did some laundry, and then vacuumed the house. Even the kitchen was cleaned, and, according to my original letter, "I picked up Linda on time."

I was sharing a Biblical teaching at my friend Candy's apartment that morning. Among the other attendees were Linda and Shirley. The four of us remained afterward to practice prophetic utterance.

The problem developed when we were ready to go our separate ways. Candy wanted a ride where Shirley was going; Shirley was in a hurry; Candy couldn't lock her apartment without us leaving first; and Linda had to use the bathroom. Solution?

God can give us thoughts to solve problems, and I believe this is one example of that. Candy gave her keys to me and jumped in Shirley's car; I gave Linda a ride home after locking up, and then picked up Candy and brought her back home. She lived only three blocks from me.

Something else that went right: a baby at that gathering had remained quiet during long prayers.

"I didn't have a lot of cash on me, but I needed a few things at Kroger's and didn't want to stop by home first. When I checked out I had ten cents left over. Cool."

Then, when I got home, Debbie (from chapter nine) and all her clients were able to go to the forest with me and our dog. We had a really nice time.

After returning from the forest, I wanted to run an errand in a nearby town. That would position me to stop at Value City Department Store, which was notoriously disorganized even though they had a huge assortment of goods. I wanted napkin rings.

Upon entering the store, I had a divine encounter. I don't know how else to explain how I happened to ask a particular girl where I might find napkin rings. She was on her way out, and one would assume she was a customer, but it turns out that not only was she an employee, but napkin rings were in her department.

I was off to a great start. The napkin rings were in boxes of four at a great price, and I found one pattern I really liked. Unfortunately, I saw only two boxes, and I wanted a set of twelve. But then I noticed two loose ones that were the same pattern. That meant there had to be two more somewhere. After searching for quite a while, I located the eleventh ring, but gave up after that and headed up to the checkout register.

But wait a minute: this is a day when everything went right. Yep, you may have guessed it. On the way to the cash register, there was another holiday display with the final napkin ring!

On the way home, I tried to share with the cashier at Ames, how God had been blessing me all day long. I have to chuckle at how that went because she didn't seem very receptive. Then she announced my total: $1.05. Huh? I thought I was undercharged, but she explained, "Half price." I just replied, "One more blessing," and left the store.

Fun Time

Have you ever had days where everything went right? If not, try recalling all the things that went right yesterday. You might be surprised.

25

The Music Side

"Reading lips, I noticed one of the ladies leaning over to her neighbor and whispering ...."

When I was growing up, there were two grand pianos at one end of the living room beneath my bedroom. I'd wake up to my mother practicing Chopin or Rachmaninoff down below me. And you can be sure no child of hers would grow up without some knowledge of music.

She had over eighty students who arrived and left, one right after the other, from 9:00 in the morning until 7:00 in the evening. In those days, anybody could be excused from school to go take a music lesson.

As a matter of fact, that's how I learned to cook! When I walked in the back door after school, she'd holler at me, "Mary, start the potatoes in the pressure cooker." I was not one to simply make do with meat and potatoes. I liked some flavor. It wasn't long before I was using the blender to concoct all sorts of salad dressings for our salads.

I remember one time how much I was enjoying my hamburger with tons of condiments. It was delicious and hard to eat because there was so much stacked. After consuming half of it, my father asked me if I'd be adding the meat. There on my plate was the entire burger, untouched.

Back to the subject of music: I decided to take up the flute. That was after the band director wouldn't let me play drums because, as he said, "Girls don't play drums." That was back in 1952. But I'm happy with the flute, and it's sure a lot easier to pack and carry around!

I had a really cool breakthrough with my flute playing right after I met Jesus in 1975. I was to perform for a music club (made up of mostly snooty lady musicians) in the town where I lived. Training my fingers to cooperate with the desired speed of a musical passage was extremely difficult for me. I'd practice some passages over and over very slowly up to twenty times a day, and then when performing, I'd fumble.

On this particular occasion, I really hadn't been practicing as much as I normally would, but I performed anyway. To my amazement, the fast passages just flowed beautifully. Reading lips, I noticed one of the ladies leaning over to her neighbor and whispering, "She's really been practicing." The truth is that I had not, but somehow the spirit of God inside me just lifted me to a new level of carefree playing. How cool is that!! Once you make Him Lord of your life, you get the added advantage of having His Spirit live inside you. It's really awesome.

I never had any desire to pursue a musical career, but I've had lots of compliments on my playing. At a local church, the pastor and his wife would rave about how sweet it was when I picked my flute up during worship. I had no idea how special it was until one Sunday morning I opened my eyes during our worship time, and there was the pastor right next to me holding a microphone and recording my flute. I was shocked.

In the Recording Studio

I love adding flute tones to another's music; I love how Holy Spirit inspires me; I love to know my music blesses others. Ron also is musical, and God inspires him as well. He can sit at the piano, or pick up his guitar, and make up a song for anyone who comes along. God works in him and downloads the words.

One time, he was playing the piano, and the Lord played a movie for him in his mind. That's how he wrote "Band of Glory," which is on one of his three albums. I also like blending in with my flute and making it up as I go. Of course, God is with me and helps me come up with the right insertions.

I see God in so much of my life. People have no idea how much fun He is.

Fun Time

When has talent in you come alive? Were you acknowledging God?

Did You Say God is Religious?

"But I wasn't prepared for the words that were to land on my page!"

I love to camp. Ron, on the other hand, was raised a city boy. As one of my friends remarked, "His kind don't camp!" However, in Ron's case, one of the stipulations that I'd marry him was that he would go camping.

Now in his mind, that would be fulfilled after one experience. In my mind, it was to be a lifestyle. We got that worked out, and we camp twice a year: once in the fall for my birthday, and once in the spring to celebrate our wedding anniversary, which is in April.

In April of 2006, Ron agreed to not only camp but also pack for the trip. That really stretched him. But eventually, we left a month after our anniversary on his birthday in May.

We left our car at the trailhead and took off with our backpacks. It was significantly late in the day, and I was concerned about finding a decently flat area where we could set up camp before dark. To make matters worse, the sky was threatening.

We found a spot, and in my haste, I shouted at Ron to tie the ropes better. Tying knots is my expertise—definitely not his. By now, not only was the sky darkening, but we could hear thunder in the distance. I was in a hurry to have cover before we got soaked, and in my impatience, my demeanor was less than kind.

We made it, stayed dry, and Ron forgave me for my crossness. I also forgave him for being so awkward.

The next morning, I settled myself next to a tree under a blue sky and took up my notebook. I love to journal, to write as I'm inspired. But I wasn't prepared for the words that were to land on my page! Here's how God dealt with me.

> *I am holy, and I am not ritualistic. Two clumsy people in the woods are a riot. One is clumsy physically; the other is clumsy mentally. Sound decisions are the way of the Lord. Make sound decisions and be blessed. Forsake the ways of the world, and learn the ways of the Lord. Remember Philippians 4:8. This is how you're supposed to think. Both of you could stand to work on this. Be kind and be strengthened in My might. I am wise and compassionate. My love is unending. I am a good listener. Covet to hear what your partner is saying. You both are treasures to Me.*
>
> *Covet to extinguish the garbage and concentrate on whom I've made you. Ask Me what to think about. Ask Me what to do. I know what will bless you both. Don't forget that I am with you in all things. I can give you expert advice in everything that you endeavor.*
>
> *Give your husband credit where he's done valiantly by his standard. Let him give you credit where you have done*

valiantly by your standard. Remember that I get the glory, and your loving tenderness to one another gives glory to Me. I have great ideas for lots of fun for you both. I also am worthy of your time and praise.

Fun Time

Have you experienced God's humor in your life? Is this a new concept?

27

Hearing from God

"'I wonder if the tires are okay.' I was looking at the right rear tire at the time."

You may have noticed in several earlier chapters that God has revealed things to me. Actually, I hear from Him daily, even though you might not have reason to believe that to be true. However, there are plenty of incidents where I've clearly gotten needed information supernaturally—for which I'm truly thankful.

In 1987, Ron and I made a trip to California to visit his brother and do some sightseeing. After a week with his brother, we left to rent a car to go exploring the second week. The following incident humorously illustrates how God got involved.

At the car rental, we got one a bit banged up. It had a dent in the side, a scrape on the back, and a stained interior. I didn't complain since it was only for a week. But while we were checking it over and writing out a list of obvious damages, so we wouldn't be charged later,

I verbalized a thought I had: "I wonder if the tires are okay." I was looking at the right rear tire at the time. Well, they appeared fine, so we left.

We then stopped and had coffee at a nearby restaurant with Ron's brother David before embarking on our tour. When we came out, I noticed that the right rear tire was low. Apparently, it had a slow leak, and I can only imagine what a bummer that would've been.

Since we hadn't actually embarked on our trip, we could easily return to the car rental. Our vehicle was quickly exchanged, and we embarked in a lovely clean white car with low mileage, without a scratch on it. The interior was a gorgeous, dark, soft blue. Earlier I had wondered if God was working in me. His response was, "Well, I told you about the tire, didn't I?" I love it!!! What would we do without our heavenly Father?

"Getting back on the river was exhilarating, but I was not in shape for such heavy water."

In Kansas, there's no white water to speak of; neither is much found in Ohio. So when we moved to West Virginia in 1988, I found myself back in canoe country, but pretty rusty.

I'd been watching my old club's newsletter and read about an outing on the Gauley River starting just below the dam at Summersville. That was reasonably close, so I called the trip coordinator and signed up. I explained my expertise by relating experiences on the Youghiogheny River, and his words included, "Well, the Gauley is a step up from the Yough, but I don't want to discourage you. Do you have float bags?"

Float bags are large inflatable plastic bags designed to fit into each end of the boat and under the thwarts, leaving only the middle of the canoe empty for the solo paddler. I decided I'd better get a set and mount them in my boat. This protects in two ways. First of all, it's much less likely to "swamp." That's when the boat fills with water, leaving the paddler with next to zero control. Secondly, if one flips, it's a lot easier to retrieve the boat.

Another important precaution is to wear a wetsuit, because the water is cold. Swimming in water under 40° F for more than ten minutes can be fatal. So, I got my gear in order, and then went to bed the night before I was to drive to meet the men below the Summersville dam. That's when I finally thought I'd better get God involved. So I asked Him, "Am I being foolish to go?" And He immediately replied, "Go part way."

The next morning, when I asked the strong seasoned men, about getting out part way down, they just looked at each other. Then finally one said that I could get out at Peters Creek, but that wasn't very far into the trip. My thought was, "Well, maybe that's all I can handle."

Today there's a road down to the river at Peters Creek, but back then to get out there meant carrying the boat up the side of a mountain and then across a reasonably long active railroad trestle before arriving at my car.

Getting back on the river was exhilarating, but I was not in shape for such heavy water. After the first time I "swam," the guys resigned themselves to the trip taking longer than expected. I was slowing them down. But we canoeists are a clan, and we stick together, and they were great at assisting me and keeping me encouraged.

I'm sure they were relieved to drop me off at Peters Creek. I was exhausted, and I was in no hurry to begin my trek up to the car. So I lay across those comfy float bags, intending to rest until I felt rejuvenated. My plan was to then carry my gear up to the car, get changed out of my wetsuit, and when I was really good and ready, I'd return for the canoe.

But I was in for a real surprise. Almost as soon as I lay back, I heard a motor. I looked up and there were two men in some sort of rigged-up off-road vehicle. I was alone. I thought about ignoring them but decided to nod. They stopped and ended up loading me, my boat, and all my gear, and then drove me through those woods up an old logging road and eventually to my car!

Do you think they were angels? It's really possible. I don't know, but I do know they were sent by God. And I told them that. They said, "We only took a notion to ride down here," and I said, "Well then, the Lord was in that notion." They replied, "You'd have been here til breakfast if we hadn't come along." They must have liked the way that sounded, because they said it at least five times.

I only know that God had me in His hands. He loves for His kids to have fun. He loves my adventurous spirit, and He especially loves to go along with me when invited. I'm sure glad I invited Him on this particular trip! Aren't you?

Fun Time

Have you had any experiences where you suspect an angel might have been involved?

The Snake and the Fish

"And of course, the snake's scales were stretched out the length of the fish inside the snake's body."

Most of my canoeing has been in nice weather. I have always loved being out on a small stream, just me, God, and my dog. Paddling solo is beautifully quiet and peaceful. The stream can be situated right in the middle of town, but somehow the bushes, as well as the fact that the stream is lower than the rest of the land, block out the noise and activity.

God has infinite ways to entertain us and/or get our attention. He can get us to the right place at the right time. On one occasion, I watched a snake eat a fish. It took no less than thirty minutes and was fascinating. I did not have a camera, so the pictures remain only in my mind and not easily shared. The snake was a bit nervous with me watching, but by the time I showed up, he had no choice but to finish his meal. His mouth was already surrounding the fish's head, and the snake's jaw was already separated, accepting the fish. The fish's diameter was about three times that of the snake. And of course, the snake's scales were stretched out the length of the fish inside the snake's body. I watched until the last of the tail fin was sticking out of his mouth. At that point, my canoe drifted over to block the view, and the snake took full advantage of it. When I got the boat back to where it was before, the snake was long gone. In spite of the current continuously trying to move my boat where I didn't want it to go, I managed to watch til the very tail end!

Fun Time

Have you noticed God's favor in your life? Perhaps you've been at the right place at the right time to enjoy a special experience orchestrated by God.

Savoring His Favor

Here's a collection of small, almost trivial, events which, seen as a whole, will give you a peek into the gentle flow of God's favor in my life. I've even questioned why I've seen so much favor. I wondered if perhaps I should be writing this as a fairy tale to children instead of you. Graham Cooke said something to the effect that if it's not too good to be true, it must not be God. This is a glimpse of the daily experiences that show God's favor. You have the same God.

"Naturally, I had to ease up on the gas a bit ...."

In 1989 I was driving uphill in Ohio. Suddenly in the middle of nowhere, with no houses around or any sign of human habitation, there was this dog just standing in the middle of my lane. He just stood there. Naturally, I had to ease up on the gas a bit, and then toward the last minute, he decided to leisurely walk off the highway to the side of the road.

As I crested the top of the hill, what did I see but Old Smokey sitting down below in full radar regalia. Did God put that dog there? Why shouldn't I believe it? He says He'll take care of us, and I had prayed for no cops when we left. If we'd look for God, we'd see Him all over the place!

"I suddenly realized that God was peeking out at me."

Sometimes it's God watching us! We were camping, and as I was sitting by the morning fire and watching the gray sky, I had an idea. I knew somewhere above all that grayness was a blue sky, so I spoke to it. I told the blue sky to show up in the name of Jesus Christ. If we understood our authority in Christ, we'd use it on the weather. Jesus did, and we're exhorted to follow Him.

Not ten minutes went by when I saw two small round pieces of blue emerge side by side in all that grayish white. It looked exactly like a pair of eyeglasses (with blue glass), and I suddenly realized that God was peeking out at me. It was hilarious!! I laughed so loudly that even our dog wondered what was happening. What a moment! It's our God! Sometimes He loves to play tricks. He's so much fun!

And it did clear up.

"I had just asked God to send me something to eat!"

There were some almonds in my bag lunch I didn't want to eat, so I stuck them on the sewing department lady's desk. You never know how something that seems insignificant could become huge for someone else.

The next day I found this note. "Dear Mary, you'll never know how much those almonds blessed me. I had just asked God to send me something to eat. Isn't God great and also those who walk His Word? I love you." (Signed Alinda)

"Individuals who instigate isolation or illusionary ideas are irritating idiots."

Ron and I were driving from an event in Massachusetts toward Cleveland, and I recall how bored we were with the thruway ride. You probably have figured out by now what I did about it. Yes, you're right. I asked God to make the ride fun somehow. Then we got the idea of brainstorming alliterations. The rule was that each line had to be a complete sentence. We wrote a line for every letter of the alphabet, and here are some of them.

Avoid agony and anxiety by always aspiring to altitudes of angels.

Beware of belligerent behavior; be buoyant with bountiful blessings.

Careful concern for Christ causes continual confidence and cancels clumsy complaining.

Deep devotions with the Divine develop desirable degrees of deliverance.

Entertaining evil establishes errant effects.

A firm foundation facilitates fulfilling forces.

Grabbing God's goodness and grace gratifies gallant goals.

Heavenly habits host healthy holidays.

Individuals who instigate isolation or illusionary ideas are irritating idiots.

Join Jesus for justification, jurisprudence, and joy.

Purposeful pursuit of positive passions produces peace.

Wisdom woos and will win wonderfully.

Exceptional exhilarating exorbitant ecstasy is executed by exalting His Excellency.

Yearn for Yahway.

"He had only been at the bar for a few minutes when he suddenly had a queasy feeling that he should leave ...."

A guy attended our home fellowship in 1989, but stuck to his normal routine of drinking beer at a local bar before going to bed. One particular night we had a prayer vigil after our regular meeting. Our new acquaintance chose to stay for the prayer time before going for his beer. He had only been at the bar for a few minutes when he suddenly had a queasy feeling that he should leave, so he did. The next morning, he learned that if he'd remained in that seat another ten minutes, he would have been the victim of a stabbing! Of course, the queasy feeling was provided by our Lord.

Evidently, God wasn't too concerned about his beer drinking. Instead, God honored his priority of putting prayer first.

"But when she arrived at the gate to leave, her name had been bumped from the computer!"

Following is from a letter dated 1989:

> A couple of weeks ago, I was extremely concerned that our Bible study be PRACTICAL. I mean, who besides

religious people enjoy Bible study? I felt an urgency for the evening study to be practical and enjoyable, and my entire body was noticing it.

Ron and I went out to eat with one of the ladies in our group, and the three of us prayed that the verses on my heart would all somehow relate themselves with each other. There were so many different topics that I wanted to expound upon all at once. Well, as usual, God had the most magnificent solution.

I got the idea just in time too. First, I'll give you some background. Two days beforehand, our friend Shirley called for prayer from the San Diego airport. She had called the airport twenty-four hours in advance and confirmed her flight. But when she arrived at the gate to leave, her name had been bumped from the computer! Oops bigtime! She told me she knew that she'd be on that plane the whole time, but she definitely was tempted with pressure. It ended up that somebody in first class canceled, and she got to ride first class.

Maybe *Somebody* knew that first-class seat would become available and chose Shirley to be the one to get it. Besides, the experience helped build her faith.

The letter continues:

When it was time for me to teach, I started out telling Shirley's airport incident as if it were some remote person and then suddenly said this was Shirley at the airport, and it only happened two days ago. Shirley was sitting right there, and after she added a couple of details, I had each person find a verse of Scripture that Shirley had obviously made her own in order to be victorious. We came up with a great assortment.

Every so often one girl exclaimed, 'This is really fun!'

We made a list of twelve different Scriptures, thus spanning all the topics I'd wanted to teach.

"It was our anniversary, ..."

This is one more example of God's favor. On a flight from Switzerland to London, I enjoyed witnessing to a man in German. Once in London, I had five hours at the airport. I wasn't going to sit there that long, but I knew I didn't have time to go into the city for a little while. This was long before all the security we have today, and I did have plenty of time to take a train from the airport to the south coast at Brighton. There I found a new dress in a used clothing store to wear on the plane home. It was our anniversary, and I was thankful that Ron could watch me getting off the plane in a new dress.

"When I woke up, I saw I'd used up my forty minutes and prepared to scoot back to the jeep. Then I noticed the horse."

It was 2016. Ron was tuning a piano at a church in some remote town of West Virginia, and I was starting to feel sleepy. I needed to drive him two hours to another location for the next two jobs. Somehow, within the next forty minutes, I had to fit in a place for our dog, Shiloh, to play and also for me to get a nap.

I would need a place close to water for Shiloh and hoped for something away from people so I could sleep without worrying about other dogs showing up to agitate her.

I started to drive toward a park on a river about ten minutes away when the thought hit me that I could turn down one of those back streets toward that same river and find something close by, saving myself a costly twenty minutes of driving time. Besides, I was dangerously sleepy.

Well, my exploration landed me at a dead end with three driveways: one straight ahead, one to the left, and one to the right. Now these were all tiny properties, mostly with mobile homes, and I could easily see there was nothing beyond except a field to the right and more properties in other directions. Also, there was a man working in the back of the house to the right. I turned the car around, but I knew he'd be curious who I was (as any stranger in these parts definitely stands out), so I rolled down my window and explained I was looking for some place where my dog could play in the river, and where I could lie down and read. (I didn't think I should say I wanted to sleep.)

Apparently, he was a very simple soul, and he said, "Well, the river is right there—pointing to it, and there's lots of grass in the field. You just drive through that gate over there." Wow, you'd never get that response around any large, populated area these days. But I was in real country, and this old fella was definitely country through and through. He just pointed me to the obvious. He seemed so sweet somehow. He had a long beard and reminded me somewhat of the Duck Dynasty look.

I threw a ball into the river a few times to get Shiloh happy, and then I lay down on my blanket for a snooze. It was a bit chilly, and my time was very limited, but the sweetness of this event just swelled to even greater dimensions.

I lay there very still, having a conversation with God. I knew He'd wake me up in time and give me the rest I needed. That's when the sun came out, and I felt this awesome warm ray of sun land on my bare shoulder. My heart swelled up with amazement, and I proclaimed, "God, You are gazing at me!" It was so softly exhilarating. And then I realized that gaze rhymes with rays, so I spoke, "God, You gaze on me and shine Your rays on me."

At that point, my peace was at the falling-asleep stage, and I was just about out when I decided to throw the ball one more time for Shiloh. I didn't have to get up as I could grab it with the ball launcher and toss it into the river from where I was lying. Next, I repeated the above process with God and fell asleep.

When I woke up, I saw I'd used up my forty minutes and prepared to scoot back to the jeep. Then I noticed the horse. I'm not sure when he showed up, but as I was picking up my blanket to fold it, he was not particularly happy with my presence and carried on with neighing at me. Shiloh was too interested in her ball to get involved.

But then I threw the ball which landed only twenty or thirty feet from the horse, and when Shiloh got to the ball, so did the horse. All this was between me and the jeep. Shiloh picked up the ball, but there she was face to face with that HUGE thing, and the horse took a notion to chase after her. Well, smart dog she was, she got out of there NOW! The horse couldn't chase her far, as she was beyond the fence in a flash. When I got past the horse, I called Shiloh, and she came right to the car.

There was something about that old man, as well as my brief communion with God that really stands out in my heart. The whole incident was so sweet. I don't think I'd ever encountered such sweetness before. It occurred to me the man was an angel.

As I left, I hollered "Thank you" to the man, and he stood there with one arm raised to acknowledge me, and I drove off.

"'Well, you tell that to this mosquito,' as she slapped one dead on her arm."

A woman who occasionally attended our fellowship called me, and I invited her to go walk in the woods with me and Poocher, our dog. To my surprise, she accepted, although the outdoors was not usually her cup of tea. She expected to sit at a picnic table and read the Bible together, but I informed her that I really intended to walk and proceeded to lead her along a path all uphill.

I walked extremely slowly so she wouldn't get bummed out and then found a nice rock to sit on once Poocher was safely away from the road. We were a bit sweaty, and the bugs loved us. Then I shared with her about the name of Jesus Christ being greater than "bugs." She was sure that she believed the Bible, but she never claimed any of the promises.

When I told her about bugs submitting to Jesus Christ, she replied, "Well, you tell that to this mosquito," as she slapped one dead on her arm. Then I took her to Philippians 2:9 and encouraged her with what GOD said about it. That verse assures us that the name of Jesus is higher than any other name. We prayed in the name of Jesus. She believed, and we sat there for forty-five minutes with no more bug attacks.

One time, a bee flew really close to my leg, and I just said, "You get out of here in the name of Jesus Christ," and it turned around and flew the other way. She was impressed. In fact, she shared about it at our fellowship the next night.

> **"It's just a detail, but after living fifty years with one 'just a detail' after another 'just a detail,' a pattern becomes apparent."**

I so love how God hooks us up with others. It seems to happen a lot, and it's always for mutual blessing.

Here's an example. Through a series of events that happened because I was preparing a surprise blessing for one friend, we ended up meeting Mike and Sandy, who lived up toward where our local outing club had planned a weekend camping trip. It rained that first night, but we got invited to stay at our new friends' home before joining the campers in the morning, thus avoiding all the rain.

It's just a detail, but after living fifty years with one "just a detail" after another "just a detail," a pattern becomes apparent. In my case, it's been a pattern of one blessing after another. How we posture our minds before God makes all the difference.

And I'm sure the blessings will continue! "All things work together for good to them that love God ..." (Romans 8:28). The "all things" includes the good and the bad. What do you posture your mind to receive? What expectations do you have? How you think directs your life.

Fun Time

Have you noticed God working in your life? Do you write down your experiences so you will be able to recall the details at a later date?

The Parenthetical Chapter

I wrote this book close to a year ago, but instead of taking the finishing steps to get it published, I paused and wrote another book. When I began to look at this one again, something very deep began to bother me. I got concerned that I might be presenting a false God, one that doesn't exist for many people. He's not Pollyanna.

Whom do you think I asked about this problem? Well, yes, I'll admit I brought it up with my husband and a couple of friends. But ultimately, I asked God Himself. His answer was not immediate, but it came. He filled me with tears of joy at this point. I am closer to Him right now than I was in the last chapter. He's real; He's infinite; He's God. Oh, if you could only get to know Him.

Have you ever heard of the word, *abba*? It's the Aramaic word for father and implies the intimacy of our English term, *daddy*. It's found three times in Scripture. One of them is in the Gospel of Mark when Jesus spoke to His Father.

And he said, Abba, Father, all things are possible unto
thee; take away this cup from me: nevertheless not what I
will, but what thou wilt.

Mark 14:36

Note the intimacy Jesus enjoyed with His Father. Note also that Jesus instructed us to follow Him (Jesus). We are to follow Jesus and walk as He walked. Doesn't that mean we should also enjoy an intimate relationship with His Father, who is also our Father?

Can you picture a good daddy with his children? Maybe they're at the ice cream parlor. Imagine the happy faces with tongues on those cones. Or maybe they're at the toy store, and they're all pointing at the toy they want. Next thing you know, they're home playing with those chosen toys. A good daddy **wants** to give to his kids. Naturally, he knows, being a good father, he can't always hand out everything they ask for, but I dare say it's more about him restraining himself when he shouldn't give rather than being relieved.

There's a section of Scripture in The Passion Translation (TPT) that stood out to me three months ago. It goes like this:

… Overwhelmed with bliss are all who entwine their
hearts in him, waiting for him to help them.

Isaiah 30:18 TPT

"Overwhelmed with bliss" is what I feel I've experienced all my life. And yet, if you read the book I just published, *Escaping Loneliness in Marriage,* you certainly would notice some non-blissful moments in my past.

If you put both books together, you might be shocked to learn that much in the previous chapters took place during those dark times of our marriage.

It is true that I positioned my mind to receive from God. It is true that how we think determines our life. It's true that God rewards all who trust Him. All of this is true. All of what you've read so far is true. But ...

There's more. There's a huge more. Continuing in Isaiah is another clue.

> ... *How compassionate he will be when he hears your cries for help! He will answer you when he hears your voice!*
> *Even though the Lord may allow you to go through a season of hardship and difficulty, he himself will be there with you. He will not hide himself from you ...*
> Isaiah 30:19, 20 TPT

Of whom are those verses speaking? Who was the Lord in the days of Isaiah? Was it Jesus? Before Jesus was introduced to the world, God took on the job description of Lordship, namely His relationship to man as Master. Now we make Jesus Lord (which is critical for salvation). Nobody knew God as Father until Jesus revealed it. Jesus introduced to the Jews that the God with whom they were familiar was more than the One they already knew. He was Father.

Ephesians 1:3 refers to the relationship between God and Jesus as Father and Son.

> *Blessed be the God and Father of our Lord Jesus Christ ...*
> Ephesians 1:3

> *How blessed is God! And what a blessing he is! He's the Father of our Master, Jesus Christ, and takes us to the high places of blessing in him.*
> Ephesians 1:3 The Message (MSG)

It has always stood out to me that it says "of," not "the." Jesus never claimed to be the Father.

...wonderful heavenly Father, the Father of our Lord Jesus ....

Ephesians 1:3 TPT

God was Father, but it wasn't until Jesus's resurrection that others could enjoy His Fatherhood. Look at verse seventeen of chapter two.

For through him we both have access by one Spirit unto the Father.

Ephesians 2:17

"Through him," Jesus, "we both," Jews and Gentiles, "have access by one Spirit unto the Father." Access!!! Access to the Father. We have access to the Father. The Father, God the Father.

Most Christians don't get that far. They stop at Jesus. Many Christians get to Jesus and never make it to the Father. Jesus is not the Father. Whom did Jesus preach? He preached the God and Lord of the Old Testament and **presented Him as our Father.**

Jesus is who He is because God the Father decreed it. God made Him King. God made Him Lord.

Therefore let all the house of Israel know assuredly, that God hath made that same Jesus, whom ye have crucified, both Lord and Christ.

Acts 2:36

Concerning his Son Jesus Christ our Lord, which was made of the seed of David according to the flesh;

And declared to be the Son of God with power, according to the spirit of holiness, by the resurrection from the dead.

Romans 1:3, 4

Jesus made Himself equal to God because He was literally God's Son. Any earthly son of earthly lords or kings was always considered to be equal to his father.

> *Therefore the Jews sought the more to kill him, because he not only had broken the sabbath, but said also that God was his Father, making himself equal with God.*
>
> John 5:18

> *That really set them off. The Jews were now not only out to expose him; they were out to kill him. Not only was he breaking the Sabbath, but he was calling God his own Father, putting himself on a level with God.*
>
> John 5:18 MSG

> *... he called God "my Father," which made him equal to God.*
>
> John 5:18 TPT

> *... because he had said of God, that he was his Father, and had equalled himself with God.*
>
> John 5:18 Murdock

> *... he was even calling God his own Father, making himself equal with God.*
>
> John 5:18 ESV

> *... he called God his Father, thereby making himself equal with God.*
>
> John 5:18 NLT

Originally, I did not intend for this book to be a deep dive into Biblical study, but I questioned what I was presenting and came to the conclusion (with the Father's help!) that it was crucial for my readers to understand what God I was experiencing all these years. I had to get to know Jesus in order to get to the Father. The experiences presented in this book are expressions of the Father's love for this child.

I urge you, dear reader, if you haven't already, to get to know the Father of your Lord. He is mighty and amazing. And He loves to bless His kids.

I have been His kid all these wonderful years, and He has thrilled me over and over (and over again). Go to the Father directly, if you haven't already, and let Him thrill your heart with sweetness.

Fun Time

Ask God to show you how to be His kid.

Monumental Memories
in Montana

"We took it but the toilet didn't work."

Our trip to Montana in 2014 was a wonderful time of sweet-ness and enjoyment. It was also a couple of weeks of one God-cidence after another. We planned to camp part of the time and stay in motels the other nights.

We looked for our first camping site near Helena. What we found was on the west slope of the continental divide with high winds, threatening thunderclouds, rain in the air, and 48°. We decided that simply showing up fulfilled our camping obligation for the time and proceeded to the Budget Inn in downtown Helena.

Our trip had begun in Missoula, where a prophet and friend had prayed that "the sun would follow us as we traveled," and that it did. After that brief shower the first night in Helena, we never saw rain again. In fact, it even dried up that very evening so we could enjoy a street party celebrating the fortieth anniversary of a local restaurant.

I always find it amazing how we just "happen" to be at the right place at the right time. I have learned that simply showing up as opposed to carefully planning via the internet ahead of time works best. The following morning, we discovered the weekly farmer's market delightfully filled with crafts and fresh foods.

History and museums were captivating in Montana. In a small town named Roundup, there was a museum that had an interesting exhibit about a local rebel celebrity pilot named David Comstock. The museum displayed an airplane he had built and flown as a teenager (along with his under-aged girlfriend). They flew at night to avoid getting into trouble, and they used Main Street in Roundup as a landing strip.

A particular tour guide named Rhea was at the Musselshell Museum when we visited. She was amazing and took to us as much as we enjoyed her. Again, it was a "God-cidence" because she worked there only one day a week. After giving us a lovely tour with special privileges, she met us after the museum closed and personally drove us out to where miners had built homes against a cliff using existing rock formations as part of the construction. In one case, the natural rock overhang was the roof. These are amazing and unique, but they are located way off the beaten path. Who would have thought we'd get all that special treatment as a result of visiting a museum?

Before you think you've got it all figured out, let me explain something. I spoke to Rhea as a fellow believer. I made the assumption that she loved God as much as I did and built the camaraderie that won her heart. People love to be approached as if they have the best values possible. (Recall the drugstore proprietor of chapter three.)

Our last outing eastbound was camping at Medicine Rocks State Park. The rocks were like nothing I'd ever seen before. (You won't be disappointed if you Google pictures of the park.)

Finding wood would have been difficult, as many campers had preceded us and cleaned out any fallen wood. But what others hadn't thought of provided us with plenty of firewood. Next to our tent site was a very large tree with a huge dead branch on it. Since we had some good rope, Ron threw it over the branch, and the two of us gave it a good tug. And there it was—lots of dead wood for our fire for both supper and breakfast. God provided once more.

On July 4 we went to a real rodeo. Montana has not only maintained the cowboy rodeo, but also the feel of the America in which I grew up. For instance, sitting in front of us was a mom with her kids, their friends, and cousins. I entertained them with videos of my dog. We were having a good time while we waited for the show. Then their mom realized she needed to run a quick errand, and instead of rounding up all the children, she simply asked me (a stranger) if I'd keep an eye on them.

We camped that evening next to a roaring, rushing brook. The next day we decided to take a hike, and we climbed part way up to Glacier Lake. Just getting to the trailhead involved eight miles of driving on bare rocks called the road.

After being on the hiking trail for a while, I encountered a mother and son on their way down. I asked if they went all the way to the lake, and she replied that after she stepped into snow up to her waist, she decided to turn around. As we were talking, another couple of guys, decked out with all their fishing gear, informed us that they not only went all the way to Glacier Lake, but over to Emerald Lake as well. Both were frozen so they didn't fish. Their comment was, "It was a nice walk, though." I will testify it was not only a nice walk, but a severely steep hike as well.

Our return trip westward included the Bear Tooth Highway,

which dips into Yellowstone Park in Wyoming. At one of the rest areas, we were intrigued with chipmunks that would eat from our hands. Since I had lots of snacks in our car, I passed out "chipmunk food" to other travelers as well.

Ron specifically said he did not want to camp that night because he wanted to be able to shave and take a shower. I wanted to camp but decided to cater to my husband's wishes. God can be really cute sometimes, and here's how He solved our night's accommodation. We found a vacant cabin (of extravagant expense). Due to the July 4th holiday, it was also the last available housing. We took it, but the toilet didn't work. They couldn't fix it, so they refunded our money. That was well and good, but everywhere we stopped there were no vacancies. Finally, we ended up erecting our tent at a primitive campground. The next morning, Ron was able to shave at a rafting company while I inquired about horseback riding. Then we went riding where a nice hot shower was provided afterward. So Ron got his wishes.

I chose a different route for "bathing." The Yellowstone River is sourced from melted snow and very cold. But I actually was able to completely submerge, and I even got somewhat used to it for a few minutes.

The next night, we found a wonderful deal: a two-bedroom house for only $90 for the night. I shopped, cooked, and prepared salads that would feed us for the remainder of the trip.

Fun Time

Before embarking on your next outing, try consciously inviting God to go along and see how it works out.

Parting Ways

"And You provide spiritual paths in unlikely places for me to enjoy with You."

In parting ways, I thought perhaps you would enjoy reading a letter I wrote to God. I was feeling a bit down on this particular day, so the letter is also an example of how I've trained my mind to switch into a posture to receive His advantages.

I wrote this during a stretch of sixty-three days when I challenged myself to type seven minutes of prophecy every day. The other sixty-two letters were sent to humans.

> *Dear God,*
>
> *Lord, sometimes I feel so inadequate. I know where I should be going, but I fail. But You never fail, and You are always there both to pick me up and cheer me on. Thank You for my husband Ron and all he means to me. Thank*

You for assuring him of Your goodness and giving him insight into how to talk to me especially when I get so messed up. Thank You for patience. I so need more of it.

Ron said the more I speak in tongues, the more patience I'll have. He said that I can be patient because You said I can do all things through Christ which strengthens me. I know You are my strength, and I know You are the One who holds me up. Thank You for being at my side, and for Your strength being mighty in me.

You enrich me on every side. You keep me functioning in glorious ways. You show me the paths on which to walk. You find physical paths in obscure places for Shiloh (our dog) and me to enjoy. You provide spiritual paths in unlikely places for me to enjoy with You. Thank You for providing those pathways to freedom. Thank You for showing me how to attain Your freedom in the midst of heaviness and oppression.

And thank You for keeping me from exploding. You are the stability on which I trust, and You are the solidarity on which I stand. You are the Rock under my feet. You spring me forward with Your charge, Your powerful charge in the spirit. You never let me stay down but always shoot me into new vistas of understanding Your ways. Your ways are higher than mine, and Your might is always at my fingertips. You enjoy my spirit, and You obliterate the dark areas in front of me.

God, Your might is my stay. Your power is my stronghold. Your glory is my seat, and Your light is my path. You shine Your glory before me and cause me to bask in Your light. Your presence is always with me, and I can soak up Your spirit at will. Thank You for being my mainstay and my might. Thank You for being my strength, both physical and spiritual.

Thank You for helping me abide in Your arms at all times. Your arms always hold me tight as I put my trust in You. I choose to trust You at all times. I choose to put my whole heart in Your ways. I choose to step out on Your promises. I choose to uphold Your word in everything I do. You are the way, and I choose to walk in it. Thank You for helping me stand strong with all my choices in Your truth.

Thank You for truth, and for teaching me how to acknowledge it more. The truth is spread out in Your Word, and You are spread across the pages. Thank You for helping me absorb Your love and truth as I peruse the Scriptures. Thank You for teaching me Your love and for helping me pursue You to a greater degree.

Show me love, God. Show me how to love in every situation. Show me how to magnify Your love as I walk in greater boldness among people of the world. Let my light shine brighter.

Okay, God, I am a patient person, and my patience extends beyond my own expectations because Your Spirit is undergirding my emotional heart. Your Spirit of the utmost mercy is at the bottom of every action I can possibly take. So, Father, I have become the epitome, the prototype of Your patience. I can be patient and extend Your mercy in every situation. You are able, and You have enabled me too. Thank You God Almighty for Your encouragement and sustenance!!

You are the mighty God, and You will stand behind every one of Your promises in Jesus's mighty name. Amen.

Fun Time

Try spending a few moments to jot a list of what God is saying to you.

Appendix One

Scriptures of Delight and Gladness

But let all your godly lovers be glad! Yes, let them all rejoice in your presence and be carried away with gladness. Let them laugh and be radiant with joy!

Psalms 68:3 TPT

Thou wilt shew me the path of life: in thy presence is fulness of joy; at thy right hand there are pleasures for evermore.

Psalms 16:11

Then shall the young women rejoice in the dance, and the young men and the old shall be merry. I will turn their mourning into joy; I will comfort them, and give them gladness for sorrow.

Jeremiah 31:13

... neither be ye sorry; for the joy of the LORD is your strength.

Nehemiah 8:10

A merry heart doeth good like a medicine: but a broken spirit drieth the bones.

Proverbs 17:22

Glory and honour are in his presence; strength and gladness are in his place.

1 Chronicles 16:27

This is the day which the LORD hath made; we will rejoice and be glad in it.

Psalms 118:24

But be ye glad and rejoice for ever in that which I create: for, behold, I create Jerusalem a rejoicing, and her people a joy.

Isaiah 65:18

Fear not, O land; be glad and rejoice: for the LORD will do great things.

Joel 2:21

And it came to pass afterward, that he went throughout every city and village, preaching and shewing the glad tidings of the kingdom of God: and the twelve were with him.

Luke 8:1

In the multitude of my thoughts within me thy comforts delight my soul.

Psalms 94:19

Thou hast loved righteousness, and hated iniquity; therefore God, even thy God, hath anointed thee with the oil of gladness above thy fellows.

Hebrews 1:9

For the kingdom of God is not meat and drink; but righteousness, and peace, and joy in the Holy Ghost.

Romans 14:17

And these things write we unto you, that your joy may be full.

1 John 1:4

Appendix Two

Scriptures for healing

He sent his word, and healed them, and delivered them from their destructions.

Psalms 107:20

I have seen numerous times when simply hearing or reading the Bible brought physical or mental healing to someone.

But if the Spirit of him that raised up Jesus from the dead dwell in you, he that raised up Christ from the dead shall also quicken your mortal bodies by his Spirit that dwelleth in you.

Romans 8:11

The word *quicken* is old English for "to make alive." I was acquainted with one lady who had rheumatic fever and, after reading this verse, she suddenly realized that God intended for New Testament believers to be healed. This is because she found it in the Book of Romans. It specifically says "mortal bodies," so there's no room for explaining this to mean anything other than the fact that Christian believers should expect God to heal their physical bodies. This revelation set her free, and she lived many more years without rheumatic fever.

… neither be ye sorry; for the joy of the LORD is your strength.

Nehemiah 8:10

Sometimes leaning in on God's joy brings physical well-being. There have been times when I felt my energy level subsiding, and I would simply declare this phrase from Nehemiah, and my energy surged. The joy of the Lord is one's strength indeed.

A merry heart doeth good like a medicine: but a broken spirit drieth the bones.
Proverbs 17:22

Verily, verily, I say unto you, He that believeth on me, the works that I do shall he do also; and greater works than these shall he do; because I go unto my Father.
John 14:12

Certainly, this would mean that healing is included. The following verse in Philippians would also include physical healing.

But my God shall supply all your need according to his riches in glory by Christ Jesus.

Philippians 4:19

Who his own self bare our sins in his own body on the tree, that we, being dead to sins, should live unto righteousness: by whose stripes ye were healed.
1 Peter 2:24

This verse, as well as Matthew 8:17, was quoted from the Book of Isaiah. Isaiah 53:5 ends with, "… and with his stripes we are healed." In this Old Testament verse, it is a prophecy.

That it might be fulfilled which was spoken by Esaias the prophet, saying, Himself took our infirmities, and bare our sicknesses.

Matthew 8:17

"Esaias," of course, is Isaiah. Matthew is declaring that Isaiah's words are being fulfilled. By the time it's written in I Peter, it's already a done deal, hence, the past tense: "… by whose stripes ye *were* healed." [emphasis mine]

Healing is always available to one who believes. Never give up praying.

About the Author

Best-selling author Mary L. Gordon lives in southwestern Pennsylvania with her husband Ron, not too far from the river of Chapter Twenty-Seven. They have been married thirty-eight years and together they enjoy ballroom dancing, musical performing, eating Mary's exotic cooking, and hiking. They also continue to combine canoeing, camping, and backpacking.

Mary brought two nephews and a niece into the marriage, and today they enjoy eight "grand" nieces and nephews scattered in various locations: Nebraska, Indiana, and southern Louisiana.

Most mornings, Mary loves to sit on her bean bag chair on top of their floor bed where she reads the Bible and enjoys God's presence and input. That's where she journals and writes her books. God always shows up, and she claims His presence often enters through her favorite windows.

Beautiful Windows

You probably noticed a few poems in this book. God downloads some of her journaling in poetic format. She finds it delightful. Her book, *Inspired Moments of Truth, A Book of Poetry* is a collection of many of those poems. She says she will need to publish a second collection as God has provided her new favorites since then.

Ron loves to tune pianos and has made that their livelihood. He also sings, and together they perform for nursing homes, churches, and parties. Ron has recorded three albums of his own original music. Mary plays flute on each of them.

Ron and Mary's marriage began in darkness even though both of them were committed Christians at the time of their wedding. Her book, *Escaping Loneliness in Marriage, 5 Crucial Concepts to Feel Loved in a Volatile Marriage* will give you wonderful insight into their lives, how they changed from desperation to love, and the keys to enable you to do the same.

Both Ron and Mary are serious Bible students, and Ron published his first book entitled, *A Deeper Understanding of Biblical Concepts.* They love to host Bible events in their home.

Resources and Websites

The poems and jingles of chapter eleven can be found in Mary's book *Inspired Moments of Truth, A Book of Poetry*.
www.inspiredmomentsoftruth.com

The book *Escaping Loneliness in Marriage* mentioned in Chapter Twenty-Nine A can be found on Amazon. More information about it is at www.escapinglonelinessinmarriage.com

Barbara Parlow, the artist from Chapter One, can be reached via email at: barbaraparlow@aol.com. She has lovely paintings for sale.

Ron's piano tuning website is at
www.gordonpianoservice.com

Visit Gordon Piano Service

To listen to Ron and Mary's music, go to www.solo.to/marygordon. Here you will find a list of links for all of the above and more, including the YouTube channel with Ron's albums. There is also a link to a YouTube channel where their dog Shiloh's tricks are displayed on short videos.

To contact Ron concerning his book, *A Deeper Understanding of Biblical Concepts*, please send email to rongordon515@gmail.com.

Other Books by
Mary L. and Ronald D. Gordon

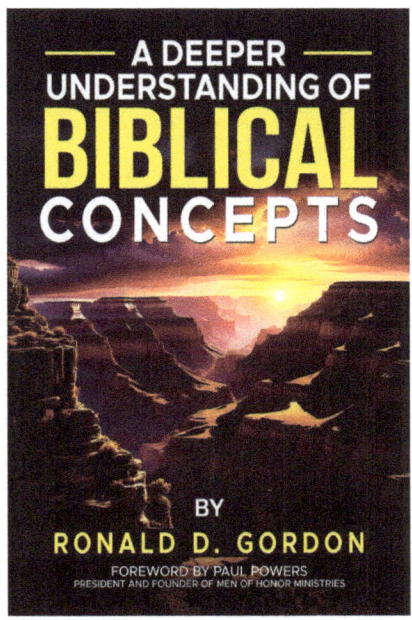

www.ingramcontent.com/pod-product-compliance
Lightning Source LLC
Chambersburg PA
CBHW051200120626
46547CB00012B/1140